Eros, Naturally

Marie-Louise von Franz, Honorary Patron

**Studies in Jungian Psychology
by Jungian Analysts**

Daryl Sharp, General Editor

EROS, NATURALLY
Jungian Notes
from Underground

with
Sett In My Ways:
A Badger's Tail

DARYL SHARP

For Bo Peep, Rebecca/Sophia, and Anthony Stevens.
Note: Some material here originally appeared in the author's other works.
Thanks to Library of America for the Emerson passages.

Library and Archives Canada Cataloging in Publication

Sharp, Daryl, 1936-
Eros, Naturally: Jungian Notes from Underground, with *Sett In My Ways (A Badger's Tail)* / Daryl Sharp.

(Studies in Jungian psychology by Jungian analysts: 139)
Includes bibliographical references and index.

ISBN 978-1-894574-41-9

1. Typology (Psychology) 2. Jungian psychology. I. Title.
II. Series: Studies in Jungian psychology by Jungian analysts, 139.

BF698.3.S52 2013   155.2'644   C2013-902779-0

INNER CITY BOOKS
Box 1271, Station Q, Toronto, ON M4T 2P4, Canada.
Telephone (416) 927-0355 / Fax (416) 924-1814
Toll-free (Canada and U.S.): Tel. 1-888-927-0355 / Fax 1-888-924-1814
Web site: www.innercitybooks.net / E-mail: booksales@innercitybooks.net

Honorary Patron: Marie-Louise von Franz.
Publisher and General Editor: Daryl Sharp.
Associate Editor: Frith Luton.
Senior Editor: Victoria B. Cowan.
Office Manager: Scott Milligen.

INNER CITY BOOKS was founded in 1980 to promote the
understanding and practical application of the work of C. G. Jung.

Cover: "Mandala One," mixed media collage, 2012, by Julian Sharp, age 7.

Printed and bound in Canada by Thistle Printing Limited.

CONTENTS

See final pages for other Inner City titles and how to order

ILLUSTRATIONS

Preface
TIPS FOR BADGER WATCHERS

A badger comes out from its sett. Will it stay out so that you can watch it? Or will it detect you and go back in?

The main thing to remember when you go badger watching is that badgers are usually frightened of people. This is because badgers have been hunted and cruelly treated by people for hundreds of years. So if a badger thinks that there are people about, it stays in its sett. This means that if you try to watch badgers at their sett, and the badgers know you are there, you probably won't see much of them.

So how might the badgers know that you are at their sett, trying to watch them? And how can you make sure that they don't know you're there?

Well, look at the photo above. It shows a badger emerging from its sett. Imagine that this badger is coming out of a sett that you are watching. What is it doing? It is looking, sniffing and listening for signs of danger. If it sees you, smells you, or hears you, it will go back in. So what you have to do when you go watching is to make sure that the badgers don't see you, smell you or hear you.

The badger's eyesight is not very good. It can't see colour, and can't see details very well. It can see shapes and movements though. So, to avoid being seen:

· Don't wear bright clothing. This will make your shape stand out.
· Don't stand too close to the sett. The closer you are, the easier it is for the badgers to see you.
· Do stand or sit where the badgers won't see your shape against the sky.
· Do keep still. If you move around, the badgers might see.

Making sure the badgers don't smell you.

· The badger's sense of smell is very, very good! However, it's not too difficult to make sure that you are not detected by Brock's nose:
· Don't walk over the badger sett or on a badger path. The badgers will be able to smell where you have been, and this may frighten them off.
· Don't stand or sit in a place where the wind is blowing from you, towards the sett. If you are looking at the sett, and you can feel the wind on your back, then the badgers will smell you when they come out.
· Do stand or sit in a place where the wind is NOT blowing from you, towards the sett.
· Even better, stand or sit in a place where the wind is blowing from the sett, towards you. (If you are looking at the sett, and you can feel the wind in your face, that's just right!)

Making sure the badgers don't hear you.

The badger's hearing is also very good. If the badgers are going to detect you, it will most likely be because they hear you. So it is very important that you keep as quiet as possible when you are watching badgers. Keeping quiet isn't too difficult, but there are so many ways you can make a noise without realising it! Here are a few ideas for keeping quiet on a badger watch:

· Don't wear a waterproof coat or jacket, or waterproof trousers. These tend to make a noise whenever you move, and this will frighten the badgers. If you need to keep warm, wear an extra jumper, or a fleece jacket – these are quieter.

· Don't take packets of sweets to eat while you are watching—opening plastic bags and taking wrappers off sweets or chocolates will make a rustling sound and scare off the badgers.

· Do try to sit or stand in a place where you will have a good view of the sett, and where you will be comfortable. If you have to move later because you are uncomfortable, or because you can't see the badgers properly, the badgers may hear you and go back underground.

· If possible, don't walk on twigs, over dry leaf litter, or through long grass. If you do, you will make a lot of noise. Try to walk where the ground is bare, or where the grass is short.

· If you take binoculars to watch the badgers with, take them out of their case *before* you get to the sett. If you take them out while you are there, the badgers may hear you.

· Don't talk when the badgers are out, or even while you are waiting for them to come out!

· Do enjoy talking about what you have seen, after you have left the sett!

It is important to remember that the things we have told you are not just for when you are at the sett watching the badgers. You also need to be careful when you approach the sett before the watch. Sometimes, badgers are out before you get to the sett. This means that you must be as quiet as possible even before you arrive at a sett, just in case. You don't want to ruin your badger watch before it has even started!

You should also be as quiet as you can when you leave the sett. You might think that once the watch is over, you don't need to worry any more. If you frighten the badgers now, it doesn't matter, as you are going home anyway. Think again! Is it fair to frighten the badgers, just because you have finished watching them? If you scare the badgers when you leave, they may go underground and stay there for some time. This means they have less time to go looking for the food they need to survive. So please think about the badgers, and leave the sett as quietly as you can after your watch.

So, now you know the basic "rules" of badger watching! If you go on a badger watch, and if everybody follows these "rules", hopefully you will have a good time, and see lots of badger activity.[1]

---

[1] Courtesy The Badger Trust, P.O. Box 708, East Grinstead, RH19 2WN, U.K. Photo and text: Steve Jackson / NFBG 2006.

1
Badger One:
SETT IN MY WAYS

It is midnight, a dark time when I really miss a loving presence. Well, what would you expect? It is always midnight in my burrow, except when the sun is about thirty degrees above the horizon, when a meager shaft of light throws rainbows through the beveled glass I installed at the entrance. When you're alone, even deciding what cereal to eat for breakfast creates anxiety. Cheerios with blueberries? Cornflakes and raspberries? Shreddies with banana? How profoundly selfish of me when millions elsewhere die every day of malnutrition, without water even. Well, you see what I mean—breakfast in the burrow is no laughing matter. And don't get me started on brunch.

I am mad. Not mad crazy but mad angry. I am disenamored of the outside world. People are not nice to each other, and crowds unSETTle me. Unconsciousness is ubiquitous up there—no end of commotion, hustle and bustle, but little consciousness. By consciousness I mean the awareness and differentiation of different factions of ourselves, like persona, ego, anima, animus, Self. This is psychological talk, as I have learned it from my patron Daemon (code-named D.) and his books explicating the ideas of the Swiss psychiatrist C. G. Jung.

There is an abundance of rational rhetoric out there, left-brain blah blah blah, but little attention to Eros—issues of relationship underlying all intercourse. It is perhaps for this reason that I not only avoid parties but also crowds of any kind; meetings of organizations, institutions and societies, clubs, etc. absolutely drive me up the proverbial wall; ennui, angst, political correctness and rudeness, etc., are everywhere. It isn't that I don't like others, it's just that one on one is my cup of tea, and even three is one too many.

Perhaps that is why I appreciate this like-minded exchange between my kindred souls in Kenneth Grahame's classic tale of woodlanders:

Presently they all sat down to luncheon together. The Mole found himself placed next to Mr. Badger, and, as the other two were still deep in river-gossip from which nothing could divert them, he took the opportunity to tell Badger how comfortable and home-like it all felt to him. 'Once well underground,' he said, 'you know exactly where you are. Nothing can happen to you, and nothing can get at you. You're entirely your own master, and you don't have to consult anybody or mind what they say. Things go on all the same overhead, and you let 'em, and don't bother about 'em. When you want to, up you go, and there the things are, waiting for you.'

The Badger simply beamed on him. 'That's exactly what I say,' he replied. 'There's no security, or peace and tranquility, except underground. And then, if your ideas get larger and you want to expand—why, a dig and a scrape, and there you are! If you feel your house is a bit too big, you stop up a hole or two, and there you are again! No builders, no tradesmen, no remarks passed on you by fellows looking over your wall, and, above all, no *weather*. Look at Rat, now. A couple of feet of flood water, and he's got to move into hired lodgings; uncomfortable, inconveniently situated, and horribly expensive. Take Toad. I say nothing against Toad Hall; quite the best house in these parts, *as* a house. But supposing a fire breaks out— where's Toad? Supposing tiles are blown off, or walls sink or crack, or windows get broken—where's Toad? Supposing the rooms are draughty— I *hate* a draught myself—where's Toad? No, up and out of doors is good enough to roam about and get one's living in; but underground to come back to at last—that's my idea of *home*.'[2]

And so, as I've said, I seldom venture out of my sett, but I hear from D. about the terrible things happening in his world, and it is beyond belief. This week alone: a mass shooting in Toronto, M26 in Colorado, traffic congestion, earthquakes, floods, mudslides, disasters of all kinds, some said to be due to "global warming," but apparently that is controversial, as is whether or not breast-feeding should be allowed in public.

I have nothing to say about the weather, but I have some experience with breasts. And now, I ask you, what is wrong with displaying those milk machines that nurtured us all from birth? I love them, modestly hidden or defiantly on display; the dispute is crazy-making. And meanwhile, every year we come closer to the dystopia pictured in the novel *1984*, in which the climate and everything else is controlled by an eye in the sky.

---

[2] *The Wind in the Willows,* pp. 133f.

In the hurly-burly extraverted upper world there is little appreciation of the quiet life, for instance reading a book instead of partying. I am completely fed up with the collective. Of course, if you were to run into me on one of my occasional sorties topside for provisions or friendship, you would not see that, for I maintain a happy face in the collective, just to fit in, as do so many others when hurting inside. If you've seen the movie *X-MEN,* you know who we are (though alas without superhuman powers).

In this hour of not quite rain, I am alone, but not by choice. My dear mate Badgerette (code name Bo Peep), went out last week foraging for button mushrooms and miso paste. She has not returned. I am devilishly anxious that something bad may have happened to her. Dear Bo Peep, my cherished one, is an innocent in the Big City, so trusting and so vulnerable. Perhaps a hunter fancies she'd make a lovely fur coat, or she fell into a sink-hole. Oh, the possibilities don't bear thinking of!

Badgers are by nature nocturnal creatures, but I occasionally have to go topside to replenish my larder. Then what do I see but raccoons and foxes, even coyotes, all badgers' mortal enemies, feasting on garbage and growing in numbers. It is enough to keep me underground.[3] I am what some psychological schools of thought might nowadays call schizoid or schizotypal, but I prefer the more benign, less clinical, term coined by Doctor Jung—*introverted.*

This means that I typically eschew gatherings in favor of more solitary pursuits, like reading or writing books, catching butterflies, collecting coins and stamps or matchbook covers, knitting sweaters, darning socks, making love, that kind of thing. Now, I don't actually do all that, but you get the point—I am not a political animal. And as you perceive by now, I mostly live a fantasy life. This is often more fun than reality, and a whole lot safer, unless a fox or a kangaroo gets a whiff of me. I take responsibility for my shadowy fantasies, but I don't have to act them out.

Dear Bo Peep. She doesn't know how adorable she is, for she eschews

---

[3] Which puts me in mind of Lynne Truss's entertaining *Talk to the Hand! The Utter Bloody Rudeness of the World Today, or Six Good Reasons to Stay Home and Bolt the Door.*

mirrors, an avoidance demanded by her first husband out of crazy jealousy. I do miss her, but why? Is she distinguishable from other lady badgers? Well, objectively, not particularly, but, yes, to my eyes for sure. I love the way she walks, sways her hips, tilts her head. I like how she looks after herself. Here, for instance, is an excerpt from her "Facial Care" notebook:

> To avoid looking as ravaged as Robert Redford and Clint Eastwood in their 70s, *must do* every day, morning and night:
>
> 1. Thoroughly wash face with warm water and quality cleanser (Dove, mandarin, eucalyptus, etc.). Rinse well and thoroughly towel dry.
>
> 2. Apply and gently rub in emolient/moisturizer (essential oils; cocoa butter; almond or avocado oil; body butter; cucumber and jasmine; warm honey nectar, etc.).[4]
>
> 3. Add makeup, if any (touch of flush or frangipani maybe); frisk lashes lightly. *Shape eyebrows but do not pluck.*

Now, I am just as vain as Bo Peep, thus I follow the same regimen, and so, in spite of my chronological age, I am sometimes mistaken for the teeny-bopper Justin Bieber. This pleases me no end, though Bo Peep loves me for who I really am.

Bo Peep has her failings. Her animus may sometimes spout collective opinions, but her feminine Sophia core often emits words of wisdom, and so I listen intently to distinguish her from him. Overall, I am besotted with Bo Peep. I would be a lesser badger without her; indeed, sometimes I wonder if I exist at all without her. I call it Eros, but it's love by any name. Ain't it true: all problems disappear in the face of love?

Although I do fret for Bo Peep's safety, I am meanwhile not entirely bereft. I have plenty books and records. One complete shelf in my sett is occupied by the *Collected Works of C. G. Jung*, another by Nietzsche, one by my patron D., another by Kafka, Kierkegaard, Samuel Beckett, Camus, Sartre, Steinbeck and so on. Other shelves contain a range of

---

[4] Emolients are also known as *humectants* (from Latin *humectare,* to wet or hydrate, from which comes the English *humid).*

CDs from baroque (Vivaldi, Bach, Beethoven) through rock and roll, blues, jazz, hip hop and avante garde classical. I may be a badger, but I am not a moron.

Now I offer my mood to you in these lyrics from an early composition by the 1960's rock group Buffalo Springfield:

It's getting to the point
Where I'm no fun anymore
I am sorry
Sometimes it hurts so badly
I must cry out loud
I am lonely
I am yours, you are mine
You are what you are
And you make it hard.

Remember what we've said and done and felt
about each other
Oh babe, have mercy
Don't let the past remind us of what we are not now
I am not dreaming.
I am yours, you are mine
You are what you are
And you make it hard.

Tearing yourself away from me now
You are free and I am crying
This does not mean I don't love you
I do, that's forever, yes and for always
I am yours, you are mine
You are what you are
And you make it hard.

Something inside is telling me that
I've got your secret. Are you still listening?
Fear is the lock, and laughter the key to your heart
And I love you.
I am yours, you are mine, you are what you are
And you make it hard.

And you make it hard.

Friday evening, Sunday in the afternoon
What have you got to lose?
Tuesday mornin', please be gone I'm tired of you.
What have you got to lose?
Can I tell it like it is? Help me I'm sufferin'
Listen to me baby. Help me I'm dyin'
It's my heart that's a sufferin', it's a dyin'
That's what I have to lose.

I've got an answer
I'm going to fly away
What have I got to lose?
Will you come see me
Thursdays and Saturdays?
What have you got to lose?

Ruby throated sparrow
Sing a song don't be long
Thrill me to the marrow
Voices of the angels ring around the moonlight
Asking me, said she so free
How can you catch the sparrow?
Lacy, lilting, lady, losing love, lamenting
Change my life, make it right
Be my lady.
Doo doo doo doo doo, doo doo doo doo doo doo
[At the end, Stephen Stills sings the following Spanish lines:]
Que linda me la traiga Cuba,
la reina de la Mar Caribe.
Cielo sol no tiene sangreahi,
y que triste que no puedo vaya,
Oh va, oh va, va.

[Loosely translated that is:]
How happy it makes me to think of Cuba,
the smiles of the Caribbean Sea,
Sunny sky has no blood, and how sad that

I'm not able to go
Oh go, oh go go.[5]

Three weeks now and Bo Peep has still not returned. I have a vivid memory of her emerging from a shower to come lie and frolic with me, shy but forthcoming. This image takes the edge off my aloneness, and keeps me from jumping offa bridge. No kidding about that.

Jung writes:

> If a man knows more than others he becomes lonely. But loneliness is not necessarily inimical to companionship, for no one is more sensitive to companionship than the lonely man, and companionship thrives only when each individual remembers his individuality and does not identify with others.
>
> It is important to have a secret, a premonition of things unknown. It fills life with something impersonal, a *numinosum*. A man who has never experienced that has missed something important. He must sense that he lives in a world which in some respect is mysterious, that things happen and can be experienced which remain inexplicable; that not everything that happens can be anticipated. The unexpected and the incredible belong in this world. Only then is life whole.[6]

And so, I am worried and lonely. Yet I grapple with the opposites: on the one hand I want Bo Peep back, on the other I like my solitude. I can move about unhampered by the whims of another. I can do whatever I want. If I choose to pursue a freckled lady badger sporting a mini-frock or short-shorts, I can do that without having to think how it might affect my mate. Did you ever see an unfrocked badgerette? Well, I am a master at that (or *was* until I was grounded by Bo Peep; I found her browsing in a meadow and she tamed my errant ways). I can watch sitcoms or Disney cartoons on the plasma TV I have in a niche in my burrow. I can drink and smoke to my heart's content, though such nasty habits do not endear

---

[5] "Suite Judy Blue Eyes." This group was later better known as Crosby, Stills & Nash (later with Neil Young.); Ascap. In fact, I first heard this song as *Sweet* Judy Blue Eyes." No mystery there, for I was dating a blue-eyed lady badger named Judy at the time.

[6] *Memories, Dreams, Reflections,* p. 356.

me to Bo Peep (or anyone else for that matter). Or I can write a book—
my memoirs, say—or a critique of Ralph Waldo Emerson's fascinating
Essays, or help D. with more explications of Jung's work.[7]

Yes, any and all of that I am free to do, and yet I long for Bo Peep's
dear presence, her smile, funky fur, sweet flesh, deep kisses; and her, so
shy but forthcoming, after loving me to pieces, tucking me in and
debouching to what she calls her "palace"—the ensuiteheart I created for
her in an adjoining burrow, with its own flush lavatory even. This cost
me a bundle, but I ask you, what's money for if not to accommodate your
loved ones?

So go figure. I live with the opposites. But don't we all? I hear from
Jung and D. that this is called conflict. And conflict is good. It is the precursor of consciousness—indeed, the *sine qua non.* Conflict tells us we
are not One but many; not masters in our house, but boarders at best, and
who the landlord is, is anybody's guess.

I have learned that any conflict constellates the problem of opposites.
Broadly speaking, "the opposites" refers to ego-consciousness and the
unconscious. This is true whether the conflict is recognized as an internal
one or not, since conflicts with other people are almost always externali-
zations of an unconscious conflict within ourselves; so long as they are
not made conscious they are acted out on others, through the unconscious
process of projection.

Whatever one's conscious attitude may be, the opposite is in the unconscious. That is Jung 101, and why the process of psychoanalysis is
seldom fruitful unless there is an active conflict. Indeed, as long as outer
life proceeds relatively smoothly, there is no need to deal with the
unconscious. But when we are troubled by trying to live with opposites,
it is wise to take it into consideration.

The classic conflict situation is one in which there is the possibility of,
or temptation to, more than one course of action. Theoretically the
options may be many, but in practice a conflict is usually between two,

---

[7] I refer to D.'s four-volume series, *Jung Uncorked: Rare Vintages from the Cellar of
Analytical Psychology* (2008-09). These are already required reading in the social studies
and psychology programs at Badger U., East York, Ontario.

each carrying its own chain of consequences. In such cases the psychological reality is that two separate personalities are involved. It is helpful to think of these as different aspects of oneself; in other words, as personifications of complexes. And thus enter shadow, persona, animus/anima and a whole host of others we never knew about.

Of course, I am not trained in such matters. I merely receive occasional echoes of what goes on in Daemon's world.

****

Now, in case you don't know much about badgers, I had better give you some facts:

Badgers are short-legged omnivores in the weasel family, *Mustelidae.* The nine species of badger, in three subfamilies, include the Melinae (badgers of Europe and Asia), *Mellivorinae* (the ratel), and *Taxideinae* (the American badger). The Asiatic stink badgers of the genus *Mydaus* were formerly included in the *Melinae* and *Mustelidae,* but recent genetic evidence indicates these are actually members of the skunk family, placing them in the taxonomic family *Mephitidae.*

Badgers include the species in the genera *Meles, Arctonyx, Taxidea* and *Mellivora.* Their lower jaws are articulated to the upper by means of transverse condyles firmly locked into long cavities of the cranium, so dislocation of the jaw is all but impossible. This enables the badgers to maintain their hold with the utmost tenacity, but limits jaw movement to hinging open and shut, or sliding from side to side without the twisting movement possible for the jaws of most mammals. Their natural predators are foxes and kangaroos, though luckily there are not too many of the latter outside the Antipodes.

Badgers have rather short, fat bodies, with short legs built for digging. Their ears are small, and they have elongated weasel-like heads. Their tails vary in length depending on species; the stink badger has a very short tail, while the ferret badger's tail can be 18 to 20 inches (46 to 51 cm) long, depending on age. They have black faces with distinctive white markings, their bodies are gray with a light-colored stripe from their head to their tail, they have dark legs with light colored stomachs. They grow to around 35 inches (89 cm) in length including tail. The European badger is one of the largest; the American badger, the hog badger and the honey badger are similar in size and weight, though generally a little smaller and lighter. The stink badgers are smaller still, and the ferret badgers are the smallest of all. They weigh around 20–24 pounds (9.1–11 kg) on average, with some Eurasian badgers weighing in at around 40 pounds (18 kg).[8]

Okay, so that may be more than you wanted to know about badgers. Not my fault. I'm just covering all the bases, you know. And in case you're wondering, I am a small honey badger. I have been known to feast on cobras, but I really prefer vegetables. I also haunt the local hives and seek out the juicy queen on her nuptial flight before she couples with her chosen drone, whom I pretend to be.[9] Now just picture that: a badger coupling with a queen bee; evolution does stretch the imagination. I can only say it helps to be a shape-shifter.

Now that calls for a tune. How about Billy Holiday?—

> You don't know what love is
> Until you've learned the meaning of the blues
> Until you've loved a love you've had to lose
> You don't know what love is
>
> You don't know how lips hurt
> Until you've kissed and had to pay the cost
> Until you've flipped your heart and you have lost
> You don't know what love is
>
> Do you know how lost heart feels
> At the thought of reminiscing?
> And how lips that taste of tears
> Lose their taste for kissing
>
> You don't know how hearts burn
> For love that cannot live yet never dies
> Until you've faced each dawn with sleepless eyes
> You don't know what love is
>
> You don't know how hearts burn

---

[8] This information was culled from various internet sites and modified.

[9] See Frith Luton, *Bees, Honey and the Hive,* pp. 137ff.

For love that cannot live yet never dies
Until you've faced each dawn with sleepless eyes
You don't know what love is

What love is.[10]

****

Now at peace after a fretful, lonely night, I scan my bookshelf for what to read. There stand Kafka's *Diaries,* but I think I've had enough of him; once exhilarating, I now find him utterly depressive. Kafka could be the cover-boy on a book about the puer aeternus, the mother-bound fella who never leaves the comfort and safety of the maternal nest. Well shit, no throwing stones; that's me too (sett = mother). Come to think of it, Daemon wrote a book about this enigmatic writer.[11] Talking about reluctance to commit himself to a loved one, here's Kafka:

> I must be alone a great deal. What I accomplished was only the result of being alone. The fear of the connection, of passing into the other. Then I'll never be alone again.[12]

All hogwash. I am a writer too (so to speak), but I would give it up for a loving and willing body. I mean, I would rather write than eat, but I would rather make love with Bo Peep, my badgerette, than eat or write. You see, even badgers have priorities.

Speaking of the tension between being outgoing or alone and inward-looking, the eminent British psychiatrist Anthony Storr offers this astute comment on the subject:

> [There are] two opposing drives in human nature: the drive toward closeness to other human beings, and the drive toward being independent and self-sufficient.[13]

Now, ain't that the truth!

Storr goes on to discuss the importance of *play* in living a creative life.

---

[10] "You Don't Know What Love Is," with a bow to Chet Baker; Ascap.

[11] *The Secret Raven: Conflict and Transformation in the Life of Franz Kafka.*

[12] *Diaries 1,* pp. 292f.

[13] *Solitude,* p. 70.

He first refers to the eminent psychologist Donald Winnicott's apt concept of "creative apperception," which depends upon linking subjective and objective, inner and outer worlds:

> It is creative apperception more than anything else that makes the individual feel that life is worth living.[14]

Storr goes on then to state that "probably there is always an element of play in creative living":

> When this playful element disappears, joy goes with it, and so does any sense of being able to innovate. Creative people not infrequently experience periods of despair in which their ability to create anything new seems to have deserted them. This is often because a particular piece of work has become invested with such overwhelming importance that it is no longer possible to play with it.[15]

I can certainly attest to that. I sometimes stay up writing until six or seven in the a.m., because I'm having such fun, but Bo Peep knows that at least half of that time is spent wringing my hands in desperation or staring at the wall, wondering what to write or do next—because such is the vanity of authors that I take my creations too seriously.

On the other hand, I may suddenly decide at two a.m. to do the dishes or the laundry (off-peak hours, energy efficient, or so they say: power smarter), or water the plants. But when I finally pack it in and turn off all the lights, Bo Peep is always there for me. I admire her, and I love her like elephant. She is the hole in my head. She doesn't own my soul, but she is a big part of it. Think about it: the heart was invented (evolved) for more than just pumping blood. That is Eros, naturally.

Daemon himself has admitted to me that he resists becoming overcompliant with external reality. But he then risks becoming solipsistic in his turret and entirely divorced from the outer world. Storr sums it up nicely, paraphrasing Winnicott:

> If the individual regards the external world merely as something to which

---

[14] Winnicott, *Playing and Reality,* p. 65.

[15] Storr, *Solitude,* pp. 70f.

he has to adapt, rather than as something in which his subjectivity can find fulfilment, his individuality disappears and his life becomes meaningless or futile.[16]

I think Storr is really on to something here. He ends his chapter on "The Hunger of Imagination" as follows:

An inner world of phantasy must be regarded as part of man's biological inheritance. Imagination is active in even the best adjusted and happiest human being; but the extent of the gap between inner and outer worlds, and hence the ease or difficulty with which the gap is bridged, varies greatly in different individuals.[17]

And just so, the person who bets on the races, buys lottery tickets or watches football on television is giving rein to fantasy although he or she may not be creating or producing anything. Indeed, hobbies and arcane interests are often aspects of a human being that most clearly define their individuality and make them the people they are.

Storr adds these relevant observations:

In Britain, every weekend sees the banks of rivers and canals lined with fishermen, who keep a discreet distance from one another, and seldom converse. Theirs is essentially a solitary sport, in which so little happens that phantasy must be particularly alive. The same applies to gardening, and to many other interests, whether obviously 'creative' or not, which occupy the leisure of those whose basic physical needs have been provided for.[18]

****

I poked my head out of the sett today for a few minutes. Jeez, what a horror: shootings in Toronto and Colorado, schoolchildren massacred in Connecticut, civil war in Syria, *e.difficile* in hospitals, floods in Haiti, fires in Australia, West Nile mosquitoes, and predictions of the end of the world next week—on December 21, 2012. I cannot bear it, so I

---

[16] Ibid., p. 72.

[17] Ibid.

[18] Ibid., p. 73.

seldom venture out. Call me an ostrich, but I am not a masochist.

My days are mostly spent on my iMac, which is not so much an addiction as a habit, but essential for business. And what is my business, you may well ask. Well, my business, pure and simple, is helping master D. sell books. He is far too busy to do that on his own.

Actually, I often can't go to bed without imagining that Bo Peep is there waiting for me. Well, I ask you now, who can?

I mean no disrespect to the homeless, or to those thousands of lonely badgers who seek companionship on dating sites. But to those encased in coital comfort, I would say, "If you were told you had only one week to live, how would you spend that time?" Think about it.

Meanwhile, enjoy the moment, for it may be your last.

****

2
Badger Two:
ALL THAT JAZZ

Hey now, and greetings. Did you actually buy all that baloney in the previous chapter? Did you believe that a badger could have a plasma TV in his sett? How did you imagine he could have paid for it, let alone tussle it into his lair? And all that guff about writing? Do you think I can touch-type with these paws and claws?

****

Anyway, I am glad to tell you that my dear Bo Peep came back today, fresh faced and as jaunty as ever, toting a basket of mixed vegetables, sweet-meats, and a little brown watering can (code named LBWC). She told me that on her way back to our lair she encountered a rogue badger who bit her feet because she refused to couple with him. Bo Peep kicked him in the knackers, her usual response to importunate advances. You see, my Bo Peep is faithful and true, she will have no other than me. Of course I find this very gratifying and instructive, for instinctively I am apt to ogle the first freckled lady badger I see rooting in the clover in skin-tight, transparent leggings. Still, I do not pursue these whimsical attractions. I always return to Bo Peep's loving arms, for she chose me among many others courting her, and her charms constantly bedazzle me. She has a divine spark. I mean, isn't that what relationship is all about? Bedazzlement, befuddlement, it's all one and the same—keeps you on your toes, trying to figure out how to live your truth without hurting anyone. And your loved one may suddenly say or do something hurtful. It's a rat's ass, but that's just how it is—Eros, naturally.

Okay, so after being reunited, we did have a minor spat last night. I say "minor," because I don't remember what it was about. Bo Peep probably doesn't either. Anyway, that's par for the course when anima meets animus. You know how it is, one sparks the other.

"I'll go back to mother," she finally cried.

Jeez, her mother died years ago. But it would be cruel to remind her.

"I'll make it up to you," I said. "I will try to be a better person."

Then I charlestoned Bo Peep around the kitchen, careful to avoid our new gas range and fridge (well, what's money for?). I put on a CD and mimed the words to her:

> Is you is or is you ain't my baby?
> The way you're actin' lately makes me doubt
> Yous is still my baby-baby
> Seems my flame in your heart's done gone out
> A woman is a creature that has always been strange
> Just when you're sure of one
> You find she's gone and made a change
> Is you is or is you ain't my baby
> Maybe baby's found somebody new
> Or is my baby still my baby true?
> Is you is or is you ain't my baby?
> The way you're actin' lately makes me doubt
> Yous is still my baby-baby
> Seems my flame in your heart's done gone out
> A woman is a creature that has always been strange
> Just when you're sure of one
> You find she's gone and made a change
> Is you is or is you ain't my baby
> Maybe baby's found somebody new
> Or is my baby still my baby true?[19]

Bo Peep squealed, "You rascal, you know I love only you!" and dragged me off to bed, countering with:

> I love you. I love you.
> Is all that I can say.
> I love you. I love you.
> The same old words I'm saying in the same old way.
> I love you. I love you.
> Three words that are divine.
> And now, my dear, I'm waitin' to hear
> The words that will make you mine.

---

[19] Lyrics by Louis Jordan, 1944; Ascap. See it on YouTube.

> Dear Badger, I love you.
> Can't you see I love you.
> I love you. Can't you see I love you.
> I love you. I love you.
> Three words that are divine.
> And now, my dear, I'm waitin' to hear
> The words that make you mine.[20]

My Bo Peep/Badgerette is especially beautiful in candlelight without her stylish but modest Parisian culottes. No one knows this but me and her former husband. Oh how I love to ruffle her funky fur and nuzzle her bare flanks. I could write a poem to her dear breasts. I am feverish just thinking of it. Bo Peep is not just a bit of fluff or a romantic fantasy. She was a singer and dancer in her prime; in another age she would have been a courtesan, shy but forthcoming. D. once told me he would rather write than eat; well, personally I'd rather make love with Bo Peep than write. I may be a solitary badger, but I am not an anchorite.[21] And I treasure our LBWC as I do our children.

To tell the actual truth, though it gives away one of our secrets, Bo Peep seduced me with the video of Kate Bush's "Wuthering Heights":

> Out on the wiley, windy moors
> We'd roll and fall in green
> You had a temper, like my jealousy
> Too hot, too greedy
> How could you leave me
> When I needed to possess you?
> I hated you, I loved you too
>
> Bad dreams in the night
> They told me I was going to lose the fight
> Leave behind my wuthering, wuthering
> Wuthering Heights.
>
> Heathcliff, it's me, Cathy, I've come home

---

[20] "I Love you," by Frank Sinatra; lyrics by Johnny Mercer and Gordon Jenkins (modified); Ascap.

[21] Anchorite = chaste religious recluse in medieval times, given to sitting on a sky-high pole for days on end.

I'm so cold, let me in-a-your window
Heathcliff, it's me, Cathy, I've come home
I'm so cold, let me in-a your-window

Oh it gets dark, it gets lonely
On the other side from you
I pine a lot, I find the lot
Falls through without you
I'm coming back love, cruel Heathcliff
My one dream, my only master
Too long I roam in the night
I'm coming back to his side to put it right
I'm coming home to wuthering, wuthering
Wuthering Heights

Heathcliff, it's me, Cathy, I've come home
I'm so cold, let me in-a your window
Heathcliff, it's me, Cathy, I've come home
I'm so cold, let me in-a-your window

Ooh let me have it, let me grab your soul away
Ooh let me have it, let me grab your soul away
You know it's me, Cathy

Heathcliff, it's me, Cathy, I've come home
I'm so cold, let me in-a-your window
Heathcliff, it's me, Cathy, I've come home
I'm so cold, let me in-a-your window
Heathcliff, it's me, Cathy, I've come home
I'm so cold.[22]

And that is Eros, naturally.

---

[22] EMI Music Inc. See Kate Bush perform it on YouTube.

3
Badger Three:
TRUTH-SAYING

"The reason there is time," opined Albert Einstein, who knew more than a little about the subject, "is so that everything doesn't happen at once."

Now, more recently, we hear from Dr. Andrew Quackenbush, professor of physics emeritus at the University of Nevada:

> Time is a euphemism for the passing of wind. Whatever happens today has already happened yesterday, and will happen again tomorrow. This is an ineluctable sequence, however we may seek to distract ourselves by making appointments or love.[23]

To tell reality, I am only a badger by night. By day I am much like you. I fret over my taxes, the laundry, the dishes, my bowels, my hurting feet; I take out the garbage, use emolients, wonder whether or not to shave, etc. I help D. sell books; for which he pays me a decent stipend. How else do you imagine I could afford vegetables and this underground sanctuary?

I read quite a lot, but almost immediately forget what I've read. You see, I am an elderly badger, underground or topside. If I didn't mark off each date on my desk calendar I wouldn't know what day it is. I worry about home invasion, kids in Somalia, the Taliban, AIDS, *e-coli,* West Nile, SARS, impotence, and falling down the stairs. I regret not learning Mandarin or Urdu, and not getting to Prague. I have a fleet of grab bars in the bathroom, reading glasses, a walker, a Lifeline button, and I am considering hearing aids. I would like to be the last badger standing.

Bo Peep nudged me, "You silly, don't be maudlin. You're only old once. Enjoy it."

Easy enough for her to say. Bo Peep is barely fifty and unafflicted by infirmities of any kind, except for her crush on me. She hasn't even had

---

[23] *Physics Today,* vol. 78, no. 2 (November 2009).

her first mid-life crisis. Never mind, I love her yet. Indeed, I do love her like elephant (which means powerfully, in case you haven't guessed).

When I was in the hospital last year recovering from acute CHF (congestive heart failure), a nurse told me that almost everyone else in that hospital was there on account of CHF, and few would ever leave. That actually made me feel better and I was discharged after ten days. I later tried to contact that nurse, a cute Philppina, with no success.

Let me introduce you to my little ones. Here are the twins, Rebecca and Sophia, now ten years old. I can hardly tell them apart, nor can they, so close it brings tears to my eyes. Then there is their younger brother, Bradford, who with ADHD is a real handful. Their mother, Bo Peep, embraces them all equally, plays no favorites. Myself, I pick and choose, according to who wants or needs more loving, including me.

Now, I realize that my Badgerette, Bo Peep, is not just a simple-minded creature of my imagination. She has her own likes and dislikes, her own complexes and hair style. Pardon me if I pretend she is my own creation, omni-available to my every wish. Not my fault. Isn't that every mammal's fantasy?

Bo Peep poked her head out. "I am a mammal," she said, "and I have no such fantasy."

"Little darling," I replied, "please don't interrupt when I'm on a roll. It's bad form."

She sniffled. "I'm hungry."

"Beloved," I said, "Rest easy, I'll just whip up some scrambled yeggs and cinnamon toast to give you pleasure."

Bo Peep lifted her lovely snout. "And just what are 'yeggs'?"

I embraced her and laughed. "I could play possum, but to say the truth, it's a concoction of what chickens lays, laced with TCP [cannabis] that I thought up in my head to make you more amenable."

Bo Peep pulled me into her private burrow, discarding her skimpy top. "You silly, come here and I'll show you *awomenable!*" And that is Eros, naturally.

I willingly submitted to her badgerette wiles, and after we showered I went back to work recording my dreams.

My dear Bo Peep, I love her, and she gives me her love so sweetly. She is the perfect image of my anima, my inner woman—so demure, shy but forthcoming. Well, I may be a badger, but I am not a monk.

****

"Trust thyself; every heart vibrates to that iron string."
—Ralph Waldo Emerson, 1848.

Okay, let's see what else we've got in the hopper today.

Years ago, I could not read two or three pages of Kafka or Nietzsche without becoming feverish. Now it is Ralph Waldo Emerson whose writing drives me into a tizzy of reflection. A page or two and I am besotted with envy for the way words flow from his quill like honey nectar from a hive. I have the questionable gift of being able to identify not only with characters in films and TV series, but also with writers as I read the words they've tugged from their minds onto a blank page.

Case in point. Here is Emerson quilling about love and relationship after being married for several years:

> Not always can flowers, pearls, poetry, protestations, nor even home in another heart, content the awful soul that dwells in clay. It arouses itself at last from these endearments, as toys, and puts on the harness, and aspires to vast and universal aims. The soul which is in the soul of each, craving a perfect beatitude detects incongruities, deficits, and disproportion in the behavior of the other. Hence arise surprise, expostulation, and pain. Yet that which drew them to each other was signs of loveliness, signs of virtue, and these virtues are there, however eclipsed. They appear and reappear, and continue to attract, but the regard changes, quits the sign, and attaches to the substance This repairs the wounded affection. Meantime, as life wears on, it proves a game of permutation and combination of all possible positions of the parties to employ all the resources of each and acquaint each with the strength and weakness of the other. For it is the nature and end of this relation that they should represent the human race to each other. All that is in the world which is or ought to be known, is cunningly wrought into the texture of man, of woman.[24]

---

[24] *Essays: First and Second Series,* p. 106.

Now, can you match that for psychological insight? No wonder Jung admired him. From the passion of first love to the recognition of the loved one's incongruities and flaws, and finally the serenity of companionship, encompassing all that is or ever has been in a relationship between man and woman. The archetypal intent for intimacy is awesomely expressed. And Emerson caps it with this observation:

> Their once flaming regard is sobered by time in either breast, and, losing in violence what it gains in extent, it becomes a thorough good understanding. They resign each other, without complaint, to the good offices which man and woman are severally appointed to discharge in time, and exchange the passion which once could not lose sight of its object, for a cheerful disengaged furtherance, whether present or absent, of each other's designs. At last they discover that all which at first drew them together—those once sacred features, that magical play of charms—was deciduous, had a prospective end, like the scaffolding by which the house was built, and the purification of the intellect and the heart, from year to year, is the real marriage, foreseen and prepared from the first, and wholly above their consciousness.[25]

Oh, such a positive view of the married state as "virtuous companionship"! For balance, as it were, put it alongside Kafka's narcissistic *cri de coeur* at the height of his first attempt to marry Felice Bauer:

> There will certainly be no one to blame if I should kill myself. … F. simply happens to be the one through whom my fate is made manifest. I can't live without her and must jump (out the window), yet … I couldn't live with her either. (D2, p. 20)

> Impossible to live with F. Intolerable living with anyone. I don't regret this; I regret the impossibility for me of not living alone. (D2, p. 157)

And definitively:

> The fear of the connection, of passing into the other. Then I'll never be alone again. (D 1, pp. 292f.)

> Jeez, what a loser.

---

[25] Ibid., pp. 106f.

****

Best things to come into the hopper today are these whimsical tidbits from Public Radio International (PRI):

1. The Chinese invented chopsticks, instead of forks, so their people would eat slowly, taking small bites, and not get indigestion. They followed this coup by genetically engineering rice down to the size of mouse turds. And to top this off, they invented Mandarin, one of the most enigmatic languages on earth. Still on a roll, they went on to write the *I Ching*. And that is why the Chinese will inevitably take over the world.

2. In the frozen north, where polar bears are all white except for a black nose, it is said that the bears, when hunting seals, put a white paw over their noses to completely blend in with the surrounding snow, thus fooling their prey. Now many scientists are occupying themselves with the question: "How does a polar bear know its nose is black?" The speculative answers range from guttural conversations between bears to the snow or ice acting as a mirror.

3. A couple in Chicago, Mr. and Mrs. Snodgrass, have paved their bedroom floor with $60,000 worth of pennies glued down, prompting interior decorators to express "pennies-envy" and questions such as: Why the bedroom? Is there some connection to their erotic life? Copper, after all, is linked mythologically with Venus, goddess of love.[26]

Not my fault. Just saying ... Or as my tomfoolery poppa, bless his soul, used to say when I pricked my finger on a rose bush, or had a rash from poison ivy, "Don't worry, son, it's better than a stick in the ear."

Or as Dude Lebowski said, "Sometimes you eats the bar, and sometimes the bar eats you." Either way, that is deep, and only the swift reach it and are delighted.

That is romance and Eros, naturally.

****

Foodists

We can no longer just eat what we enjoy or want. We are besieged by

---

[26] Okay, so I tweaked them a bit. So sue me.

celebrity chefs and recipes we can hardly understand, with ingredients only available in a local market that we don't have the means to get to. It is all very depressing, this "gastro-culture" of food. You can't have a hamburger without feeling guilty. Coffee is suspect, and so are sugar, salt and chocolate. The food culture is a fad, a bubble, a mania not so different from the eighteenth-century obsession with tulips.

****

Bye the bye, my patron and mentor D., publisher of this book, has received some pleasuring comments on his previous tome, *Miles To Go Before I Sleep*. For instance:

> Diarist extraordinaire!
> You should call it *Smiles to Go* ...
> It is a surprisingly sunny and happy book. Easily your most lyrical.[27]

****

PRI (Public Radio International)

A wonderful perk for staying up into the early morning hours is that you

---

[27] Personal communication.

[D:] 'Being called a diarist was a new idea to me, but I took it as a compliment. I like the ring of it, putting me in the company of such as Samuel Pepys (1633-1703) and perhaps even Ralph Waldo Emerson (1803-1882)—though personally I do not aspire to such acclaim. I think of myself simply as a humble scribe who has something unique to say. What I write is unprofitable. Still, I would rather write than eat, and let the reader sort wheat from chaff. I mean no offence to my readers, but I expect from them no less than what I give; that is, my all.

And this gangsta did not disappoint:

I've been re-reading *Miles To Go...* . It's an instant classic.

Well, I might have thought it, but he said it—exactly the kind of appreciation that keeps me up writing late into the early a.m.

get to listen to PRI, which broadcasts music and news from all over the world. It is extraordinary. Just now I heard that there are a dozen states in the USA that are gathering petitions to secede from the Union (aka, the United States of America). Texas, no surprise, is "ground zero" of this movement. The others are mostly those states that were part of the southern Confederacy before the friggin' Civil War. No one knows to where this movement might lead, or what the point is, especially since the U. S. constitution explicitly forbids secession. . .

I also heard an announcer in Colorado pose the question: "If smoking pot leads to heroin use, will using moisturizer lead a man to nail polish, mascara, false eyelashes and lipstick?"

Now, I think that is misogynist if not also sexist, but I have to confess that I was so impressed by the clear polish on my nails after a recent manicure that I am reconsidering my lashes.

Nevertheless, what will they think of next? And who cares? The U.S. of A, with its constitutional "right to bear arms," is out to lunch, that's a no-brainer. And our own Canadian prime minister is pretty much in lockstep with U.S. right-wing thinking, sorry to say. I won't take to the streets to fight him, though, for I am not given to public protests. I'll just write about it, because that's my way. In common with D., I am not a political animal. He has his turret, I have my sett.

However, I did absent myself from sett today for a few hours in company with my trophy colleague Rebecca. She invited me to go into the collective to see *Life of Pi* in 3-D. She had seen the film before, and we both had read the book, so we had a companionable time with bags of popcorn. And the film was fantastic and thoroughly enjoyable, thanks to the author Yann Martel and the director Ang Lee. It was absolutely realistic visually, but suffused with a magical and spiritual overtone.

Rebecca drove me there and back, bless her, for I am scared of driving in the prevailing Toronto traffic, and moreover badgers are not allowed to drive cars (or anything other than lawn-mowers).

I could go on but there is another writer's mantra: "Don't overwrite." That means, I think, stop when you're ahead.

And so to bed, with Miles Davis ringing in my ears.

Truth-Saying

****

I woke up this morning in a wonderful mood. I peaked out and the sun was shining. I turned on the radio and there were no new massacres, car crashes, tornadoes, earthquakes or mudslides. Even Syria seemed to be peaceful.

My badgerette loves me. God is in his Heaven and all is right with the world. I am caught up with work, and want to dally. I dance a jig and bring back the Al Jolson tune humming in my head:

> I'm Sitting on top of the world
> I'm rolling along
> Yes rolling along
> And I'm Quitting the blues of the world
> I'm Singing a song
> Yes Singing a song
> Glory hallelujah, I just phoned the parson
> Hey, par, get ready to call
> Just like humpty dumpty,
> I'm going to fall
>
> I'm Sitting on top of the world
> I'm rolling along
> Yes rolling along
> Don't want any millions
> I'm getting my share
> I've only got one suit (one suit)
> That's all I can wear
> A bundle of money won't make you feel gay
> A sweet little honey is making me say
>
> I'm Sitting on top of the world
> I'm rolling along
> Yes rolling along
> And I'm Quitting the blues of the world
> I'm Singing a song

Yes Singing a song
Glory hallelujah, I just phoned the parson
Hey, par, get ready to call
Just like humpty dumpty,
I'm going to fall

I'm Sitting on top of the world
I'm rolling along
Yes rolling along.

From bright thoughts I have come full circle to consider the darker side of the psyche. Badgers have one too, you know; that's Darwinism. And I'll confess it outright: I am an acolyte, as is D., of the great Swiss psychiatrist Carl Jung. I am astraddle the opposites. Anyway, here follows a snippet of what I have absorbed from Dr. Jung, and you will pardon me if you've heard it before, because it can't be heard often enough. (And for the record, I do not seek to rise above my subterranean station; I wish only for my voice to be acknowledged.)

****

Everything we are not conscious of is shadow. To the degree that we identify with a bright and blameless persona (the "I" we show to others), our shadow is correspondingly dark. The persona aims at perfection. The shadow reminds us that we are human.

Psychologically the shadow opposes and compensates the persona. Where we are concerned to put on a good front, to do what is considered by others to be proper and noble, our shadow is not.

The realization of how and when our shadow enters our life and at times takes over is a precondition for self-knowledge. The more we become conscious of our shadow's behavior and intentions, the less of a threat it is to our well-being and the more psychologically substantial we become.

In Jung's model of the psyche, the shadow, or at least its dark side, is composed of morally inferior wishes and motives, childish fantasies and resentments, etc.—all those things about ourselves we are not proud of and regularly seek to hide from others. For instance, in modern civilized societies aggression is a prominent aspect of the shadow because it is not socially acceptable; it is nipped in the bud in childhood and its expression in adult life is met with severe sanctions. The same is true of sexual behavior that deviates from the current collective norm.

By and large, then, the shadow is a hodge-podge of repressed desires and "uncivilized" impulses. It is possible to become conscious of these, but in the meantime they are projected onto others. For instance, a man who unconsciously lusts after his neighbor's wife, or flirts with a coworker, may suddenly suspect his wife of having an affair.

Just as we may mistake a real man or woman for the soul-mate we long for, so we may see our devils, our shadow, in others. This tendency is of course responsible for much acrimony in personal relationships; and on a collective level it gives rise to political polarization, wars and the ubiquitous practice of scapegoating.

On the other hand, the shadow is not only the dark underbelly of the conscious personality. It also has a bright side: aspects of ourselves that make up our unlived life—talents and abilities that have long been buried or never conscious—part and parcel of who we were meant to be. They are potentially available and their conscious realization may become an exciting journey that often releases a surprising amount of energy for everyday life.

****

To bring it all home, I think Bo Peep's shadow would be mean-spirited, opinionated and withholding, everything she is apparently not. And what about mine? In two words, outgoing and lascivious—a puer like Razr, as my patron D. describes that adulterous rogue in some of his "Jungian romances." On the positive side, in the process of analysis with D., I uncovered a hitherto dormant talent for the written word and an instinctive love of Latin. I have capitalized on this ever since.

I get email in my burrow. Yes, Wi-Fi is everywhere, gnawing our brains out and searing our eyes and ears with radon or whatever they call it these days. Life is not healthy; indeed, it is downright deadly.

I get messages from young female badgers seeking a sugar-daddy. I respond politely but I don't bite. Unlike some badgers (or D.'s side-kick

Razr, see below), I don't see every passing female as a potential lover. I am true blue to Bo Peep, give or take a natural, instinctive attraction to a deep cleavage, short-shorts and see-through leggings. You see, I need Bo Peep to stay grounded. And possibly vice versa. Call it co-dependency or enmeshment or whatever you want, it's all upper-world jargon to me. I know that Bo Peep is more or less a romantic fantasy, but it's the only one I have. So sue me.

Pardon me if you've heard this too before, but it bears repeating. Every badger has an inner badgerette that he may one day meet in the guise of a winsome Bo Peep who loves him to pieces, and vice versa. No badger or -ette is so homely or misshapen that he or she cannot hook the heart of another. And it works best not to be too transparent to one another—leave enough space to fill it with one's own self; that, I am persuaded, is the bright side of projection.

They may couple and fill their house with the scampering of little badgers, and life goes on, though not always in harmony. In the course of intimacy, projections may fall away and the not-so-lovable other side of the loved one may surface—jealous, vindictive and ill tempered. This is not negative thinking, it is real life in every burrow.

****

Hearing aids

Some time ago, Bo Peep encouraged me to try these things because I kept asking her to repeat herself. Well, I spent most of this week trying to get used to them, and it's not working. Either I don't insert them at the correct angle, or they get clogged up with wax. The amplified ambient noise is very annoying; I can turn that off with the remote volume control, but then conversations are mushy or foggy. The audio graphs say I have a hearing loss. That's why I'm going through this exercise, with a 90-day approval period or money back. I thought that for 5,500 badger dollars I could expect an improvement in my hearing. You think that kind of money is easy to come by in a sett? Well, no, it's a real sacrifice, and now in order to hear at all I have to take these damned plugs out! I think the real problem is that people mumble and slur their words, and that's why I don't understand what they're saying.

And yet I fear facing the pretty audiologist with my experience. For after all, she is on commission and has her own little ones to feed.

Okay, I have another two weeks before I see her again. I'll keep experimenting before I call it quits, I owe her that much. Well, I am a real sucker for pretty audiologists. I may be a badger, but I'm not a eunuch. And the fear of a woman's wrath is the flip side of my so-called positive mother complex. That is life as I know it, and on the whole it ain't too bad.

As indicated earlier, I am disenamored of the upper world. It is undifferentiated chaos, unmitigated turmoil. It is a friggin' Blitz out there, every day, from dawn to dusk and beyond. No one is safe, not in car, on foot, on bike. Indeed, it makes me crazy. Even D. has given up his beloved harvest gold VW GTI/VR6, a zippy runabout. Myself, I hardly dare to venture out for fresh fruit and veg, or the errant garden snake. Well, I am an older badger; I don't need much but noodles, eggs, miso, peanut butter and Corn Flakes. I am encouraged by Bo Peep, however, to add steamed vegetables to my diet.

4
Daemon One:
From Sett to Turret

Jan. 2, 2013. It is my birthday. I am way past retirement age and "best before" date. But what else would I be doing on my birthday if not what I like doing best—trying to write a book? I will see my grown-up kids for dinner, but meanwhile I have cleared the decks for the day in order to concentrate on this work, which I realize no one is waiting for except me. But that's okay; it's just the way it is.

Love what you love, and let the ferryman Charon await his coinage to row you across the river Styx.

Jung appeared to me in a dream last night. This is not in itself remarkable, for thousands report dreaming of him every night. But in my dream he was in a daemonic guise, which rather puzzled me until my colleague Rebecca/Sophia suggested it could be compensation for my high regard for Jung—e.g., taking him off a pedestal. Well, I can live with that.

****

Now, there is a serious thrust, or intent, to this book, though you'd hardly know it, the way I let Badger carry on. This is not my fault. I am controlled by higher forces, call it God or a Supreme Being or whatever else you name your inner daimon. I mean, I am a mere pawn in the chess game of life—the grand scheme of things—as aren't we all? I don't mean to start a religious debate here, Biblical lore vs. evolution, I'm just saying how I feel.

Anyway, I am glad to have a chance to speak my own mind at last. And about time! I guess Badger is as much fun as one can expect from a burrowing beast, but it is not what I had in mind when I began writing this book. I thought I would model it on Dostoyevsky's cynical *Notes from Underground,* but Badger, a creature/complex of my psyche hitherto unknown, hijacked me as soon as I began. He was quite unforeseen, and so I am more than a bit befuddled.

Indeed, I hardly know what to say now, since Badger has used my best lines and tunes, and he has even co-opted my relationship with my sweetheart, Bo Peep, as if his badger-brain could encompass romance and such a passion. He is a plagiarist and a badass. I have an office on the second floor; he is under the basement. That says something. But think of the old alchemical dictum: "What is above also is below."

****

Okay, on the one hand I have the lascivious Razr (see below, chapter 8), and on the other there is this feckless trickster Badger prone to quote from my favorite authors, but who in actual fact doesn't know his arse from a sett in the ground. Pardon the cliché, but it fits. And so I live with opposites, as don't we all?

Badger is little more than a poseur, a wannabe writer—wannabe rich, famous, recognized. He veils this ambition with contempt for the upper world, without which he could not exist. I think he is evincing the onset of mental palsy, nowadays known as dementia. Leaving a person outside overnight in a blizzard has been tried in such cases, but the only treatment I know that works is a severe blow to the back of the head and a kick in the pants. Jeez, I invented Bo Peep. Badger appropriated from me the whole concept of Badgerette, yet apparently he believes he actually has a relationship with this figment of his imagination. He loves a phantom; I know the real thing. Both could be called Eros, naturally.

And so, I wonder, where am I in all this? My iMac has just tolled midnight (it actually speaks the hour, on the hour, every hour), and I am so tired my eyes feel like walnuts. What, you think it's fun being a writer? I could be outside in healthy air building a snowman instead of sewing words into sentences like an indentured factory worker in New Delhi. But I am driven. I persevere because I am Canadian, and I am stubbornly intent on writing a book. That is what we call being complexed.

For those who came late to this party, a complex is a cluster of emotions associated with a particular subject or object; hence the expressions "mother complex" and "father complex." We don't actually have complexes; they have us. Complexes are behind most of the commotion in our lives and they are especially disruptive in relationships.

For the love of women

There is no call for a man's Special Lady to get her knickers in a panshard because he confesses to loving women in general. I mean give me a break! He chose her, didn't he? She should count herself lucky to be picked out of many and not left waiting for Prince Charming. And you can't fight City Hall (i.e., instinct).

Now, I feel obliged to bring my mentor Jung into this discourse, front and center, for it is he who grounds me.

Let us start with his comments on love at an advanced age (86):

> The fact forces itself on my attention that beside the field of reflection there is another equally broad if not broader area in which rational under-standing and rational modes of representation find scarcely anything they are able to grasp. This is the realm of Eros. In classical times, when such things were properly understood, Eros was considered a god whose divini-ty transcended our human limits and who therefore could neither be com-prehended nor represented in any way. I might, as many before me have attempted to do, venture an approach to this daimon whose range of activi-ty extends from the endless spaces of the heavens to the dark abysses of hell, but I falter before the task of finding the language which might ade-quately express the incalculable paradoxes of love. I falter before the task of finding the language which might adequately express the incalculable paradoxes of love.
>
> Eros is a *kosmogonos,* a creator and father-mother of all higher con-sciousness. I sometimes feel that Paul's words—"Though I speak with the tongues of men and of angels and have not love"—might well be the first condition of all cognition and quintessence of divinity itself. Whatever the learned interpretation may be of the sentence "God is love," the words af-firm the *complexio oppositorum* of the Godhead. In my medical experi-ence as well as in my own life I have again and again been faced with the mystery of love, and have never been able to explain what it is. ... We cannot discuss one idea of it without also discussing the other. No lan-guage is adequate to this paradox Whatever one can say, no words can ex-press the whole. To speak of partial aspects is always too much or too little, for only the whole is meaningful. Love "bears all things" and "en-dures all things" (1 Cor. 13:7) These words say all there is to be said; nothing can be added to them. For we are in the deepest sense the victim

and the instruments of cosmogonic "love." ... Man can try to name love, showering upon it all the names at his command, and still he will involve himself in endless self-deceptions. If he possesses a grain of wisdom, he will lay down his arms and name the unknown by the more unknown—*ignotum par ignotius*—that is, by the name of God. That is a confession of his subjection, his imperfection, and his dependence, but at the same time a testimony to his freedom to choose between truth and error.[28]

Whew! Where to go from there? *Kosmogonos* means not of this world; *complexio oppositorum* means a complicated business—e.g., Badger can adore Bo Peep while at the same time questioning his relationship with her and coveting other badgerettes. Or indeed, that any relationship may vacillate between the opposites. You have to stand on your head to get your mind around that.

And Jung himself, although his principal paramour was apparently his wealthy wife Emma (with whom he had five children, and she became an analyst herself), is alleged to have strayed into the arms of others. I grant you, it is possible and conceivable in that era, but there is so far no convincing evidence of Jung's infidelities, if any, other than his longstanding and open relationship with analyst Toni Wolff.

Now, in Jung's published works there are no allusions to his personal life, unless you count this rather surprising remark in a letter to Freud:

> The prerequisite for a good marriage, it seems to me, is the license to be unfaithful.[29]

****

For a musical perspective on this love business, here is ol' Blue Eyes:

> I was a hum-drum person
> Leading a life apart
> When love flew in through my window wide
> And quickened my hum-drum heart
> Love flew in through my window
> I was so happy then

---

[28] *Memories, Dreams, Reflections,* pp. 353f.

[29] 30 January, 1910, in William McGuire, ed., *The Freud/Jung Letters*, p. 289. The question is, was he serious or is this comment self-serving?

But after love had stayed a little while
Love flew out again

What is this thing called love?
This funny thing called love?
Just who can solve its mystery?
Why should it make a fool of me?
I saw you there one wonderful day
You took my heart and threw my heart away
That's why I ask the Lawd up in Heaven above
What is this thing called love?

You gave me days of sunshine
You gave me nights of cheer
You made my life an enchanted dream
'Til somebody else came near
Somebody else came near you
I felt the winter's chill
And now I sit and wonder night and day
Why I love you still?[30]

Anyway, the proposed publication of Jung's correspondence with his first patient, the winsome and vastly talented Sabina Spielrein (later to become a Freudian psychoanalyst), may change our view of him. Her own diaries (dramatized in the documentary *My Name Was Sabina Spielrein),* do suggest a relationship closer than doctor-patient.

Still, David Cronenberg's film, *A Dangerous Method*, is an embarrassing travesty, implying that Jung's therapeutic approach to mental illness involved spanking. Good God, what will his detractors come up with next!? That film is not even informative about Jung's relationship with Freud and how they influenced each other.

Personally, during forty years of analytic practice, I have never spanked a client, though I once wanted to. So sue me ...

Logos and Eros

Before proceeding into deeper waters, I should differentiate these two

---

[30] Sinatra, "What Is This Thing Called Love?" music and lyrics by Cole Porter; Ascap.

concepts or approaches to life. In short, Logos is characterized by the rational, "scientific" left-brain thinking that has prevailed in the Western world since the Renaissance. Eros, while not disdaining thinking, focuses rather on right-brain values—feelings, the imagination and relationship.[31] Here in a tidy nutshell is the difference in practice:

Logos: "I think I love her."
Eros: "I love him. I feel it!"

"Love is like riding a horse or speaking French; if you don't learn it when you're young it's hard to get the hang of it later."[32]

World's end

The "end of the world" brouhaha, scheduled for December 21, 2012, has now passed, predictably, without more than the usual incidents— suicides, rapes, shootings, strikes, accidents, etc. Indeed, it is reliably reported that it was a hoax perpetrated by Big Business, especially the makers of Corn Flakes (Kellogg's) and the oil cartel—so people would stockpile cereal and fill up their cars with gasoline. No definitive motive has yet been discovered, but the FBI and CIA are said to have their best Keystone Kops looking into it.

****

I live alone. When my wife of 22 years fell in love with a glassblower and left me some fifteen yeas ago, I felt bereft. At first I put some energy into finding a new mate. Younger women were eager and willing, but they understandably wanted a future with babies, and I did not like the idea of founding another family, even accidentally.

Also, although my somewhat younger wife and I had been sexually quite active, I could not imagine a woman more or less my own age wanting to engage in the sweaty act of making love. The very thought of it seemed somehow unlikely and even obscene. So much for the

---

[31] Curiously, Eros, while known to the ancients as a male god, has in modern times become closely associated with the feminine, compensating masculine Logos.

[32] I picked up this pithy dictum from "Lord Shrimpy" in the British TV series *Downton Abbey,* season 3, episode 10. He says love, but I hear Eros, naturally.

influence on me of the cultural stereotype of older women.

Until, that is, I met Mavis, a pre-funeral advisor at the cemetery I chose to process my eventual demise. Mavis was a native of the Philippines, a five-foot, black-haired bundle of joy. At 75, twice divorced, Mavis was as frisky as a 25-year-old, and three times as inventive. She absolutely adored making love, and we spent many an adventurous afternoon tearing each other's clothes off and exploring our limits.

Unfortunately, Mavis died just before her 80th birthday, though not deliberately as did Ruth Gordon in that enchanting film *Harold and Maude*. No, she died during surgery for an acute embolism in her leg.

That was three years ago now, and I have been alone in my turret ever since, where it is hot but not sweaty. I did romance some other older women until they said they were no longer interested in "all that stuff" and offered a chaste hug and friendship instead, which in fact I gladly accepted, for women generally know a lot more about Eros than men do, and I like their company.

And aw shucks, I have pretty much lost interest in sex myself.

****

My mother

Oddly enough, when I was young, I think under ten, I used to imagine my mom was a Lithuanian gypsy. Now, I don't know where I got that idea, perhaps from a comic book or my alcoholic uncle George, her wayward brother, but it died away when I realized that she was just an ordinary, caring woman devoted to her family and getting me off to school full of porridge and a lunch bag with baloney sandwiches and a banana or an apple, orange, etc. Well, you know what I mean. She was simply a great mom, and when my forehead was split by an errant baseball bat, she sat with me in the hospital for three days, night and day, I loved her so fiercely that my regular trick was to sneak up behind her as she stood cooking at the stove and untie her apron. She'd say, "Scat! You're such a nuisance," and then give me a tremendous hug.

So, talk about a positive mother complex.

Okay, enough of that nonsense. What we should be considering is the shadow side of our Western civilization, its hidden underbelly, if you will. Shadow activities are ubiquitous in our culture, from cheating on tax returns to coveting our neighbor's wife. This reality generally only becomes apparent when celebrities, politicians or priests appear in the news for having abused the trust of their spouses, acolytes or constituents. But no man or woman is immune from shadowy thoughts that might well become actions.

****

Ah, those were the days. I mean literally—when I did yoga, and after a few minutes standing on my head, made love with the cute young teacher. But that was in Zurich. Back in Toronto, I did yoga and pilates, but the teacher was beyond flirting with and I was bored out of my skull. I always felt like a fish out of water and so I went back to writing and chiropractic. I then felt good, focusing on Eros, naturally.

Okay, so I have had the occasional lover, why not, but nothing serious enough to take me out of my solitude. I have my turret, Badger has his sett, and we both have Bo Peep. That's just the way it is.

My Zurich yoga teacher actually came to visit me in Toronto. She was a very pretty and affectionate Swiss lass, simple but not stupid. Although we frolicked in the rooftop swimming pool (of the apartment block where I lived), I was not a grown-up puer then, so I could not commit to loving her as she needed.

I do adore women. I am fascinated by them, and so I regularly become romantically involved, especially if they are beyond child-bearing age or married. It's a rat's ass, but a just so story. In spite of my best intentions, I have a habit of falling in love with women who are married or otherwise attached. I don't know what to do about this except to attend to my dreams and listen to romantic ballads on the subject, like this classic:

> Love is a many splendored thing
> It's the April rose that only grows in the early spring
> Love is nature's way of giving a reason to be living
> The golden crown that makes a man a king
>
> Once on a high and windy hill
> In the morning mist two lovers kissed and the world stood still

Then your fingers touched my silent heart and taught it how to sing
Yes, true love's a many splendored thing

Once on a high and windy hill
In the morning mist two lovers kissed and the world stood still
Then your fingers touched my silent heart and taught it how to sing
Yes, true love's a many splendored thing

Love is a many splendored thing
It's the April rose that only grows in the early spring
Love is nature's way of giving a reason to be living
The golden crown that makes a man a king

Once on a high and windy hill
In the morning mist two lovers kissed and the world stood still
Then your fingers touched my silent heart and taught it how to sing
Yes, true love's a many splendored thing

Once on a high and windy hill
In the morning mist two lovers kissed and the world stood still
Then your fingers touched my silent heart and taught it how to sing
Yes, true love's a many splendored thing.[33]

Well, let Badger stew with his furry-flanked, imaginary Bo Peep. I have my own cherished loverNot, code-name Rebecca, who is the sunshine of my life. More later. And don't let the blues make you sad.

I don't get out much lately, what with the inclement weather and having a cold. But I still get a lot of exercise; in my three-storey house plus basement I walk 3-4 miles a day up and down the stairs. I only use the stair lifts in extremis.

Holiness

I have just been listening to the Beatles, still my favorite rock group ever, and musing about how many holes it takes to fill the Albert Hall (the premier concert palace in London, UK). No kidding. This has been a question on many lips since the Beatles voiced it in 1965:

---

[33] Frank Sinatra, "Love Is a Many Splendored Thing," words and music by Cole Porter; Ascap.

I read the news today oh, boy
About a lucky man who made the grade
And though the news was rather sad
Well, I just had to laugh
I saw the photograph
He blew his mind out in a car
He didn't notice that the lights had changed
A crowd of people stood and stared
They'd seen his face before
Nobody was really sure if he was from the House of Lords

I saw a film today oh, boy
The English army had just won the war
A crowd of people turned away
But I just had to look
Having read the book
I'd love to turn you on.

Woke up, fell out of bed
Dragged a comb across my head
Found my way downstairs and drank a cup
And looking up, I noticed I was late
Found my coat and grabbed my hat
Made the bus in seconds flat
Found my way upstairs and had a smoke
And somebody spoke and I went into a dream
Ah

I read the news today oh, boy
Four thousand holes in Blackburn, Lancashire
And though the holes were rather small
They had to count them all
Now they know how many holes it takes to fill the Albert Hall
I'd love to turn you on.[34]

****

---

[34] "A Day in the Life," on *Sgt. Pepper's Lonely Hearts Club Band* (1967), lyrics by John Lennon and Paul McCartney; Ascap.

Writing

When I am working on a new manuscript, I am always writing, whether on the computer or simply honing sentences in my head as I walk around the block or try to sleep or eat alone in a restaurant—as this morning, where my waitress in the *Fox and Fondle* pub shamelessly sported a short-short plaid skirt and knee-high transparent leggings.

I had another dream of Jung last night. In this one he was a medical doctor attending to my ills. When he had finished, I asked how much I owed. He replied, "Oh, how about three times the spring in your step?"

Well, now, that's as enigmatic a remark as any I've heard in or out of dreams, and it got me to wondering just how much a spring in the step is worth—$10, a hundred? A thousand? I decided it is priceless.

****

Rejection

The feisty Gertrude Stein was a powerful literary voice in the early twentieth century. Her work, both poetry and prose, was admired in France, but misunderstood or ignored in the rest of Europe. Later, her work was widely appreciated by North American readers.

Stein is perhaps best known nowadays for her offhand utterance (in a poem) that "a rose is a rose is a rose." I mean that is so succinct, it brings tears to the eyes, and is much mimicked one way or another.

Now, in my early years I endured numerous rejections of my work, and so did Ms. Stein, but none so delightful as the gem on the opposite page, which adroitly spoofs her style without addressing the substance of her submission.[35]

Kindly forgive my brevity, for I cannot begin to encompass the scope of Stein's whimsical imagery.

---

[35] It has been suggested that the piece in question was "The Making of Americans" (1925).

FROM ARTHUR C. FIFIELD, PUBLISHER,
13, CLIFFORD'S INN, LONDON, E.C.
TELEPHONE 14430 CENTRAL.

April 19 1912.

Dear Madam,

I am only one, only one, only one. Only one being, one at the same time. Not two, not three, only one. Only one life to live, only sixty minutes in one hour. Only one pair of eyes. Only one brain. Only one being. Being only one, having only one pair of eyes, having only one time, having only one life, I cannot read your M.S. three or four times. Not even one time. Only one look, only one look is enough. Hardly one copy would sell here. Hardly one. Hardly one.

Many thanks. I am returning the M.S. by registered post. Only one M.S. by one post.

Sincerely yours,

Miss Gertrude Stein,
27 Rue de Fleurus,
Paris,
France.

Now, I plucked this letter off the internet, so it is not very legible. Here is how it reads:

FROM ARTHUR C. FIFIELD, PUBLISHER,
13, CLIFFORD'S INN, LONDON, E.C
TELEPHONE 14430 CENTRAL

April 19, 1912.

Dear Madame,

I am only one, only one, only one. Only one being, one at the same time. Not two, not three, only one. Only one life to live, only sixty minutes in one hour. Only one pair of eyes. Only one brain. Only one being, being only one, having only one pair of eyes, having only one time, having only one life, I cannot read your M.S. three or four times. Not even one time. Only one look, only one look is enough. Hardly one copy would sell here. Hardly one. Hardly one.

Many thanks. I am returning the M.S. by registered post. Only one M.S. by one post.

Sincerely yours,

A. C. Fifield

[To]

Miss Gertrude Stein
27 Rue de Fleurue,
Paris,
France.

****

Inertia

I just can't seem to get movin' … stuck in a rut, plug up my butt, can't watch smut, want a woman, but don't have the energy to go out looking.

I write, watch movies, listen to music, waste time. Bleak house, feel like a mouse, a louse. Life's a merry-go-round, as the Swiss folk hero Til Eulenspiegel discovered. He rejoiced as he toiled up a mountain, for he knew he'd soon be going down the other side, and he wept as he went down, knowing the steep haul ahead. That's life. It's another rat's ass, but that's just the way it is.

We get used to it and don't jump offa bridge. At least that's the way I see it, my philosophy, if it can be so called.

Gap-toothed

I am thinking of seventeen things at once, and don't know where to turn next. So I resort to my teeth. A few days ago I had a brawl with a crusty piece of bread *(un batard)*. I surrendered when one of my front teeth took the fall. Now I look like a hillbilly in the film *Deliverance* until I get to the dentist. Meanwhile I dare not smile and eat mostly porridge and soup.

While I Gently Weep

I spent an hour today with a financial advisor, and came away wondering how you can trust a man who wears both suspenders and a belt? And moreover sports a handlebar moustache as if he were the Sherriff of Tombstone.

I decided to put my extra cash in a sock and bury it in the back yard. As the comely 80-year-old Maude (Ruth Gordon) declares in *Harold and Maude* when she throws into the lake the love-band 19-year Harold (Bud Cort) had punched out for her in an amusement arcade: "Now I'll always know where it is."

That's when, watching *Harold and Maude* once or twice a year, I start to cry, and don't stop until Harold, after hearing from the doctor that Maude can't be saved from her birthday suicide, drives his hearse offa cliff and then dances to the closing tune by Cat Stevens:

> Well
> if you want to sing out
> sing out.
> And if you want to be free
> be free.
> 'Cause there's a million things to be.
> You know that there are.
> And if you want to live high
> live high.
> And if you want to live low

live low.
'Cause there's a million ways to go.
You know that there are.

You can do what you want.
The opportunity's on.
And if you find a new way
you can do it today.
You can make it all true.
And you can make it undo
you see.)
Ah, it's easy.
Ah
you only need to know.
Well if you want to say yes
say yes.
And if you want to say no
say no.
Cause there's a million ways to go.
You know that there are.
And if you want to be me
be me.
And if you want to be you
be you.
Cause there's a million things to do.
You know that there are.[36]

Indeed, *Harold and Maude,* the whole film, is an excellent example of Eros, naturally, including Harold's mock suicides in order to attract his socialite mother's (Vivian Pickles') attention or shock the proper young ladies she sets him up with.

****

---

[36] "If You Want to Sing Out, Sing Out," on *Tea for the Tillerman*; Ascap.

Harrod's, London UK

It is 1959. I am desperate for work, having left Paris on the Channel ferry with about $50 in travelers' checks. I roam the streets of London and stumble upon this famous department store, Harrod's. Brashly I enquire for the personnel department where I am confronted by a huge matron who requests my resumé. I hand it over, and apparently my degree in journalism impresses her enough to employ me in the book department—packing orders to be mailed out.

I really liked that job. It was puer paradise. There was no stress at all, and in our 15-minute breaks we got to go on the roof and make out with pretty secretaries who were usually keen to hook up with a Canadian to take them away from their dead-end life. Well, fat chance with me, a young stud just rampant to make love as often as possible, but unlikely to whisk anyone off to my homeland.

Anyway, one of these roof-top dollies invites me to visit her in Tottenham Court Road. I find my way there on a borrowed bicycle, and betimes, after her spaghetti au gratin and a bottle of cheap rosé we fall into her narrow bed. I was 23 and it was fun making out with a hot young lass. Atypically, she denies wanting me to take her back to Canada and make babies. "I just wanted the shag," she says. Well, bless her honesty. I don't remember her name, but I do wonder whatever became of her.

Oh, how well I remember riding the tube, the Underground, from my cot in Earl's Court to Knightsbridge, then a short walk on a crowded street to my job at Harrod's for the princely wage of one shilling, eight pence an hour and no relief except those two 15-minute breaks on the roof. It was demeaning and finally more than I could bear, and so I sought out "supply" (substitute) teaching in "secondary modern schools," which actually turned out to be much worse than packing books, though it paid better. With no training in classroom control, teaching these disadvantaged young mobsters was in fact the most dispiriting experience of my life. All the same, I have a vivid memory of a 15-year-old scrambling up to me in the midst of classroom mayhem and pleading, "Stick with it, Sir, we don't want to lose you!"

And so I left the blackboard jungle and went back to being a struggling writer in a seventeeth-century country cottage, buying vegetables with my wife's inherited dividends of about $30 a month, barely enough to live on. We had three little ones by then, and I was distraught at not being able to adequately care for them They were hard times, no doubt about that. It was the 1960s, and I found solace in the Beatles:

> Yesterday, all my troubles seemed so far away
> Now it looks as though they're here to stay
> Oh, I believe in yesterday.

> Suddenly, I'm not half the man I used to be,
> There's a shadow hanging over me.
> Oh, yesterday came suddenly.

> Why she had to go I don't know she wouldn't say.
> I said something wrong, now I long for yesterday.

> Yesterday, love was such an easy game to play.
> Now I need a place to hide away.
> Oh, I believe in yesterday.

Fast forward to 1969

Much in between, but finally we are back in Canada, in a suburb of Toronto, living in my wife Jane's inherited old house. I am very unhappy because she assigns to me the role of handyman, and that is so totally not me. I am completely overtaken by rock music and the contemporary Eros/drug culture. I grow marijuana (dubbed Belltower Fineglow) in the garden behind the corn, and smoke it in the basement. I am a decent father but not a great husband. I do freelance editing for publishers, and in 1970 I am hired as the first director of the Toronto Playwrights Co-Op. In 1971 I fly to San Francisco to visit artist friends for a month. Well, I am always more or less stoned in SF, and happily, though somewhat accidentally, I acquire an artist-girlfriend, though I am too unconscious to appreciate her. And after all I am umbilically attached to my wife by my mother complex.

Back home, Jane and I are at extreme odds. I philander at random with willing women, and she has a boyfriend she thinks I don't know about. I don't blame her for anything, but I think we both need therapy. She resists, putting her faith in astrology. I am at my wit's end, stoned half the time, suicidally depressed and conflicted. I know I am a really good candidate for Jungian analysis, but there are no Jungians in Canada at this time, so I think of going back to England, and say so.

Jane goes up the wall at the very idea. How is she to manage on her own with three kids?

We finally have a definitive set-to one night in the bedroom. I want to make up, and she says she doesn't like me anymore. I am devastated.

It is about 10 in the p.m. by then, and I am crying my eyes out. I know I have to leave, and I make that tough choice. I go upstairs to embrace my kids and tell them I am leaving; not their fault. At 7, 9 and 12, they hardly know what is happening. It is the hardest thing I've ever had to do. Some might think it selfish, but I saw it as a sacrifice in order to save myself and, eventually, them. I think it all worked out for the best in the long run, but I know they were scarred by my absence, and so I still feel a twinge of guilt.

I know there is a bus into Toronto passing by at 11 p.m., and I am on it, tears streaming down my face.

By the following week I am in London, seeing an analyst. After six months I go to Zurich and apply for training. I am accepted as a candidate, but not to begin until the following year.

I return to Toronto and bide the time in a seedy basement apartment, which soon becomes papered with my drawings of mandalas and dream images. Occasionally I see Jane and the kids, and in the fall of 1974 I begin a 4-year stint training in Zurich. I am ecstatic at the opportunity to put myself together, and incidentally become disco king of the Institute, where nothing is expected of me except to become conscious.

****

Grave-coded

I have been involved in pre-planning my funeral lately, a rather sobering experience, so I was bemused to hear on PRI of a Danish sculptor's idea to chisel the story of a person's life into a bar-code, then transfer this to a tombstone. Now I ask you, what will they think of next?

Anyway, I will be cremated, ashes sprinkled in a rose garden. There is provision for a small plaque and one line. Let my epitaph read simply:

He was kind and generous; he loved women.

Eros along the way

Okay, so I have had my fair share of badgerettes, so to speak, from my buxom teenage sweetheart in Ottawa to a lumpen middle-aged hausfrau in the Swiss Alps. With the former I was quite at sea; with the latter I felt entirely free to be me, and she rewarded me handsomely. I also remember the sweet German lass I deflowered in a pond near Munich after she picked me up on her bicycle, and her sister whom I unfrocked in the back seat of a rented VW Beetle. And I still dream of lovely Cynthia who came to clear leaves from my eaves and stayed to give me a lesson in whoreticulture. And who could forget the fetching Gretchen, who picked me up as I was hitchhiking south from Venice? We stopped for the night and shared a bed, but her pudendum was zippered tighter than the Suez Canal. I did eventually, about 3 a.m., coax her into relaxing her pelvic muscles, and in the morning she thanked me for bringing her back to life.

Oh, to be young and virile again...devil-may-care puer and unconscious of it. Jung and Zurich showed me the light, but I am still a long way from reaching it.

****

Consider the Beatles' "Yellow Submarine." The music is so captivating that the lyrics (by Ringo Starr) are seldom given their due. Here they are:

In the town where I was born
Lived a man who sailed to sea
And he told us of his life
In the land of submarines

So we sailed on to the sun
Till we found a sea of green
And we lived beneath the waves
In our yellow submarine

We all live in a yellow submarine
Yellow submarine, yellow submarine

We all live in a yellow submarine
Yellow submarine, yellow submarine

And our friends are all aboard
Many more of them live next door
And the band begins to play

We all live in a yellow submarine
Yellow submarine, yellow submarine
We all live in a yellow submarine
Yellow submarine, yellow submarine

[Full speed ahead Mr. Boatswain, full speed ahead
Full speed ahead it is, Sgt.
Cut the cable, drop the cable
Aye, aye, Sir, aye, aye
Captain, captain]

As we live a life of ease
Every one of us has all we need
(One of us, has all we need)
Sky of blue and sea of green
(Sky of blue, sea of green)
In our yellow submarine
(In our yellow, submarine, aha)
We all live in a yellow submarine
A yellow submarine, yellow submarine
We all live in a yellow submarine
A yellow submarine, yellow submarine

We all live in a yellow submarine
Yellow submarine, yellow submarine
We all live in a yellow submarine
Yellow submarine, yellow submarine.

I hear "submarine" as a metaphor for, or analogous to, my turret or Badger's sett. We human beings are generally isolated one from another. We may couple and jog together, but we are essentially alone. It's another rat's ass, but not my fault ... just the messenger.

****

Helping hand

I was feeling overwhelmed with work recently, wishing I had an assistant, and so I contacted the local journalism school to see if one of their

61

students might be available for an unpaid internship/practicum with our small independent publishing house. I had in mind an experienced, sexy, unattached woman over forty. Well, call me sexist.

Anyway, who turns up but a perky 26-year-old, an Aubrey Hepburn look-alike.

"I'm Mary Jane, I'm here to learn what you do," she smiles at 9 a.m. on a Monday. "I hope not to disappoint you."

I mean, she is so pretty that I am agog. I keep my cool, but slip into my alter-ego.

"Call me Razr," I say, "Come along now, I'll show you where you will work," as I lead her up to the third-floor self-contained suite with sitting room overlooking the swimming pool. I plug in my new Mac Air and show her how to clean our mailing list from returned catalogues.

Mary Jane is quite taken aback. She looks around in wonder at the powder room and bedroom, "Mr. Razr," she cries, "this is terrific!"

Mary Jane turns out to be a great help, keeping track of foreign rights contracts, reconciling bank statements and other things I am too jaded or lazy to do.

Two months passed. One evening, around 3 in the a.m., I had enough Scotch in me to feel impulsive and bold.

"Mary Jane," I called up the stairs, "Are you still awake? Come down here, I would like to molest you."

Mary Jane made her way down the stairs, flounced her dirndl skirt and jumped into my arms. "Oh, Mr. Razr, I thought you'd never ask!"

Well, I have a wide futon in my office, and there I cuddled Mary Jane to our mutual delight.

When business picked up, I could afford to hire Mary Jane, not at a handsome salary, to be sure, but the perks—room and board and Razr— were apparently satisfactory until she left a year later to have babies with a banjo player.

The Killing Field

Want a thrill? Watch *Kill Bill* in two volumes, Quentin Tarantino's most operatic film to date, and to my mind his best ever.

Kill Bill is essentially a bloody revenge film, a cross between a spaghetti western and *King Lear*. Spoiler alert, it involves the story of "The Bride" (Uma Thurman) awakening from a coma four-odd years after being shot in the face at her wedding rehearsal by her former lover, Bill (David Carradine). And she is 8-months pregnant. ... Thurman emerges from the hospital seeking revenge on her former colleagues, the Viper Assassination Squad. She flies to Okinowa, where she acquires a newly minted, deadly Hansai sword (traditionally used by Samurai) with which she proceeds one way or another to destroy everyone in her way as she moves from Japan to the Mohave Desert with invincible, unrelenting fury to avenge the wrong done to her.

There are many unforgettable highlights in these two movies, including Thurman's balletic swordplay in besting Sophie Fatale (Julie Dreyfus) and demolishing a small army of Japanese swordsmen and blinding Elle Driver (Daryl Hannah). She even bare-knuckles her way out of a coffin after being buried alive, a skill she learned under the harsh, tyrannical tutelage of Pau Mei, Kung Fu master who despises women but nevertheless teaches her the "five-finger exploding heart touch."

The denouement of this exciting pair of films comes when Thurman at last confronts Bill, the exquisitely evil Carradine (in the role of his life) who not only tried to kill her (out of jealousy) but also snatched the unborn baby from her womb as she lay comatose. Thurman's reunion with her cute four-year-old D.D., after delivering to Carradine the fatal heart-exploding blow, is redemptive and expunges the previous violence from the viewer's mind.

Want a thrill? Watch *Kill Bill*. It is high camp, opera and ballet, a comic book from Hell, all in one incendiary bundle. The entire cast is unforgettable, and the impressive, evocative musical score by Robert Rodriguez is worth listening to on its own as it pays homage, pastiche-like, to spaghetti-film director Sergio Leone, composer Ennio Morricone and Clint Eastwood's swagger through desert gunfights.

Walking for God

I also heard this morning on PRI the story of a man in Delaware who felt he lacked meaning in his life. Call him Wayne. He had a comfortable job, friends and a decent life-style, but they weren't enough. He had read about a religious woman walking penniless around the world for forty years, and the idea somehow appealed to him. So Wayne gave away all his belongings, bid a tearful good-bye to his girlfriend, cleaned out his bank account—put the money in a paper bag to give to a charity along the way—and spray-painted a tee-shirt with PILGRIMAGE FOR GOD on the front, and DELAWARE TO SAN FRANCISCO on the back. And so on a sunny day in November he started walking.

I need not recount the details of Wayne's ill-fated journey. Suffice to say the weather soon turned nasty and he lasted only three days without food, shelter and adequate clothing. Townsfolk shunned him, called him a bum. "Get a job," they cried. He ate radishes and slept in fields under tractors. The turning point came as he was trudging along in Maryland when he saw (or hallucinated; he wasn't sure) a giant billboard proclaiming, "Have you made a mistake? The Lord works in mysterious ways."

Wayne thereupon phoned his mom, who contacted a friend in New York to go and rescue him. Thereafter, he settled back into his mundane job and thanked the Lord for showing him the light. He never again wished to be free of the accouterments of modern life. "Been there, done that," he'd say to himself when he felt low, "and it didn't work."

Now isn't Wayne a bit like you and me? Modern life can be fun, but sometimes it is just too much—things to do, people to see, places to go, appointments to keep—and it can drive you bonkers. You are then obliged to reassess your values—what is important to you: your job? Your mate? Your clothes? Your car? It is possible to make choices. Where does your energy want to go?

When this happens, we are wont to call it a midlife crisis and it is, at any age. (I heard recently of an accomplished young woman, barely 32, who interrupted her prestigious Ph.D. to seek meaning in a communal think-tank with like-minded friends in a Central American jungle.) What to do about it varies from one person to another—divorce, a new job, new city, new friends—but always there is just the same person you were, only in different circumstances. You might think of ending this cycle by jumping offa bridge or in front of a subway train. But these moves are unappealing and sound too messy. So when a friend suggests seeing his therapist you jump at it.

Now, as it happens (if you haven't already guessed), the friend is in analysis with a Jungian who agrees to see you in her home office, so right away you feel comfortable spilling your guts to a stranger—your doubts and fears, your hopes, your dark thoughts, your feelings. There is no couch; you sit face to face and she listens. You tell her things you've never told anyone else, even yourself. She doesn't say much, but when you're stuck for words she asks about your dreams. Well shit, you could talk all day about your dreams, better say nightmares, where you are chased all over the place by featureless beings. She asks about your associations to the images in your dreams and she amplifies them with analogies in religion, mythology and fairy tales. Well, eat my socks, you always thought fairy tales were for kids and myths were the stuff of comic books—Superman, Captain Marvel, Spiderman and so on.

You leave that first hour a bit light-headed and bemused, for you feel as if a burden has been lifted from your shoulders. You walk with a new spring in your step. You feel good. You call your partner and invite her, or him, for dinner at your favorite bistro. You are singing to yourself, "I'm sittin' on top of the world ..."

Well, that is the experience of many when they first enter analysis. It is a unique experience to have the undivided attention of someone who clearly cares to hear what you have to say. You have friends you can talk to when in need, but they are not objective and they have their own problems. A Jungian analyst has been trained to put aside her or his own troubles, and complexes, and focus on you. That is refreshing, like a warm shower.

The analytic process has often been likened to a cleansing bath. Here is analyst Marie-Louise von Franz, esteemed doyenne until, and still, after her death in 1998:

> In many dreams the analytical process is likened to taking a bath and analysis is often compared with washing or bathing. In German you talk of "washing someone's head," i.e., scolding them, or showing them where they are wrong in their ideas. Most people when they come to analysis have an awkward feeling that something of the kind is necessary and that

their sins might come out. Thus the idea of a bath is a very obvious simile. The dirt that covers the body might mean psychological influences in the surroundings which have contaminated the original personality.

Of course, this raises the question of what "psychological influences in the surroundings" might "contaminate" one's personality? Good question, wish I'd thought of it first. Von Franz writes the following:

> It is much easier to be oneself and natural if one lives alone. Introverts are very sensitive and often say that they are all right when alone but that with other people they pick up disturbing influences and lose their inner serenity. All patients are not ambitious, but if one patient makes a move to do something the others all want to do the same. That is the phenomenon of mass psychology, and here primitive emotions prevail. Reason is wiped out by infection and less educated people contaminate others and all are pulled down. If one has the same potentiality that is immediately activated. As soon as you enter the human herd you deteriorate and your own shadow is activated from outside, but one can also really pick up darkness that is not one's own. People get lured into attitudes that are not theirs, and when they have time to think they wonder what happened to them. That is something we have to clean up again and again, and so we generally interpret the bath as the need to work through shadow problems. [37]

Well, we are all influenced by our culture; there is no escaping that, whether it means "keeping up with the Joneses" or simply coveting the woman next door or the latest gadget touted to make our lives easier or more fun. To those I would add the spoken or implicit injunctions to be active, ambitious, to be "out there," buying or protesting in the streets against what irks us politically—in short, we are immersed in an extraverted culture that by its very nature contaminates everyone.

Irked natives

As I write this, Ms. Theresa Spence, chief of the northern Ontario aboriginal community of Attawapiskat is on a hunger strike until the Prime Minister and Governor-General (as representative of the Queen) agree to meet her and discuss the pervasive problems on native reserves across

---

[37] *Redemption Motifs in Fairy Tales,* pp. 24f.

Canada—poverty, water quality, suicides, inadequate housing and education, and much more. A nation-wide movement called "Idle No More" has sprung up in sympathy with Chief Spence. Groups of Indians and Inuit parade in the streets, drumming their demands, or blockade roads. Nobody feels happy about this; and collectively there seems to be a consensus that Canada's native population has been ignored or underfunded for decades, if not centuries, since the "First Nations" signed a Treaty with the British Crown 250 years ago in exchange for $8 a head and the assurance that their vast lands (much larger than the size of France) would be theirs to hunt and fish in perpetuity. In the meantime their lands have been unilaterally appropriated by commercial mining and forestry concerns, with no economic benefit to the indigenous population.

These foolish things

I am apt to do some silly things in order to unfetter my otherwise flaccid imagination. To wit: Last month I put this ad in the local newspaper –

WANTED

Frisky lady older than 45 to have fun with,
from Scrabble to cruises to cuddling.
Reply to Razr, P.O. Box 5000, Toronto.

—and my box has been full ever since. I'd heard rumors, but I really didn't know there were so many lonely older women out there.

Back story: I had been diagnosed with *pudendum absconditum* (lost lover, with a Latin twist), a rare condition hitherto known only among salesmen in Arizona and Nebraska. Anyway, I never opened the many responses, having no time to sort wheat from chaff. Never mind, my condition is not contagious and has a half-life of just two months.

What's new?

Well, last night I dreamed that I was flirting with a younger woman (about 40) who said her name was YAHUDA. Thinking of Yehudi Menuin, I guessed Israeli, and she smiled. As we became more intimate she admitted that she was a Mossad special ops agent detailed to report on my activities and attitudes. And finally, when we were fully engaged in making love, she cried out, "Goy-man, I am yours. Elohim, forgive me!"

I took that to be some kind of love-cry in the wilderness, which I genuinely shared and appreciated, but I withdrew my loving attention in time not to propose marriage.

You see that solitude is not all Scotch and roses. There is a dark side to almost everything.

Well, I don't mean to brag, but I am a twenty-minute man, and I never seduced a woman who didn't invite me into her parlor. Well, okay, once or twice, in the interest of scientific research, I was more assertive than my putative partner. But Katzemjammer, that's only about two percent of my amours, and who's counting anyway?

Now, I don't mean to make myself out to be some kind of modern Don Juan, but pretty ladies, hitherto chaste, have been known to fall at my feet with their hair in disarray. Not my fault. Just saying.

6
Daemon Two:
BETTER LATE THAN SORRY

Well now, although I might have in mind the Stephen Leacock Medal for Humour, I am not writing a comic book. Badger and funny business have their place, but it behooves me to infuse this tome with more gravitas.

I suppose it is clear by now that I trained in the school of thought espoused by the Swiss psychiatrist C. G. Jung. I do not presume that all readers of this book know what such a vocation involves, so to make it simple, if I were asked to cite one remark by Jung that informs my life and attitude as an analyst, this would be it:

Only what is oneself has the power to heal.[38]

That's it in a nutshell. The whole process is there, including the idea that neurosis is an attempt at self-cure. And what is really oneself can only be discovered, I believe, through a conflict between opposites and holding the tension until the "third"—something not logically given—manifests. This typically takes the form of a symbol, but how this third, the so-called transcendent function, makes itself known depends on individual psychology and circumstances. For some it is an epiphany; for others it is a new passion or an old one rediscovered. But in Jung's model of the psyche, it always represents the creative intervention and guidance of the Self, archetype of wholeness, which functions as the regulating center of the personality.

In plainer words, the Self is a transpersonal power that is beyond the control of the ego. It can be experienced, but it is not easily defined. In short, there is no difference between the Self as an experiential psychological reality and the religious concept of a supreme being, except that the traditional Christian idea of God places Him somewhere "out there." In Jung's model of the psyche, the Self is inside. In one definition, he describes the Self as both the center and the circumference of the psyche.

---

[38] *Two Essays on Analytic Psychology,*CW 7, par. 258. (CW refers throughout to *The Collected Works of C. G. Jung.*)

Here are some significant comments by Jung on the Self:

Intellectually the Self is no more than a psychological concept, a construct that serves to express an unknowable essence which we cannot grasp as such, since by definition it transcends our powers of comprehension. It might equally well be called the "God within."[39]

Sensing the Self as something irrational, as an indefinable existent, to which the ego is neither opposed nor subjected, but merely attached, and about which it revolves very much as the earth revolves round the sun— thus we come to the goal of individuation.[40]

So long as the Self is unconscious, it corresponds to Freud's superego and is a source of perpetual moral conflict If, however, it is withdrawn from projection and is no longer identical with public opinion, then one is truly one's own yea and nay. The Self then functions as a union of opposites and thus constitutes the most immediate experience of the Divine which it is psychologically possible to imagine.[41]

Like any archetype, the essential nature of the Self (or God) is unknown and possibly unknowable, but its many and various manifestations—archetypal images—are known to us in one form or another as the content of dreams, myth and legend. Jung says it all:

The Self appears in dreams, myths, and fairytales in the figure of the "supraordinate personality," such as a king, hero prophet, saviour, etc. or in the form of a totality symbol, such as the circle, square, *quadratura circuli,* cross, etc. When it represents a *complexio oppositorum,* a union of opposites, it can appear as a united duality, in the form, for instance, of *tao* as the interplay of *yang* and *yin,* or of the hostile brothers or of the hero and his adversary (arch-enemy, dragon), Faust and Mephistopheles, etc. Empirically, therefore the Self appears as a play of light and shadow, although conceived as a totality and unity in which the opposites are united.[42]

Psychologically, uniting the opposites involves first recognizing them

---

[39] Ibid., par. 399.

[40] Ibid., par. 405.

[41] "Transformation Symbolism in the Mass," *Psychology and Religion,* CW 11, par. 396.

[42] "Definitions," *Psychological Types,* CW 6, par. 790.

in whatever conflict we are engaged in, and then holding the tension between them. The extent to which we are successful in this difficult and often lengthy endeavor—the degree of wholeness we experience—can be called a manifestation of the Self, or, if one prefers, the grace of God.

****

Now, you can appreciate the scope of Jung's ideas, and you can read everything he ever wrote, but the real opportunity offered by analytical psychology only becomes apparent when you go into personal analysis. That's when Jung's potentially healing message stops being merely an interesting idea and becomes an experiential reality. As Jung says:

> Analysis should release an experience that grips us or falls upon us from above, an experience that has substance and body such as those things which occurred to the ancients. If I were going to symbolize it I would choose the Annunciation.[43]

Analysis is not a suitable discipline for everyone, nor do all benefit from it or need it. Indeed, there may be as many ways of practicing Jungian analysis as there are analysts, but the process itself facilitates healing because it relates what is going on in the unconscious to what is happening in everyday life. That is Eros, naturally.

We generally seek a quick fix to our problems. We want an answer, a prescription; we want our pain to be treated, our suffering relieved. We want a solution, and we look for it from an outside authority. This is a legitimate expectation for many physical ills, but it simply doesn't work with psychological problems, where you are obliged to take personal responsibility for the way things are. Then you have to consider your shadow—and everyone else's—and all the other complexes that drive you and your loved ones up the wall.

Jungian analysis is not about improving yourself or making you a better person. It is about becoming conscious of who you are, including your strengths and weaknesses. I do not mean to coax you into analysis, but I want everyone to know that it is not something that's done to you.

---

[43] *Jung Seminar 1925*, p. 111.

Analysis is a joint effort by two people focused on trying to understand what makes you tick. It involves a good deal of time and energy and it can cost a lot. It generally involves some sacrifices in other areas of life, so it is a matter of priorities—you put your money, your energy, into what you value and, if you hurt enough, you find a way.

Just last week I asked a middle-aged single mother, "I like seeing you, but how can you afford these sessions?"

She smiled, "I care for my kids, but also for myself. I can manage."

I am seeing her at a reduced rate, but still … just saying.

****

My funny Valentine, sweet comic Valentine
You make me smile with my heart
Your looks are laughable, unphotographable
Yet, you're my favorite work of art

Is your figure less than Greek?
Is your mouth a little weak?
When you open it to speak
Are you smart?

But don't change your hair for me
Not if you care for me
Stay little Valentine, stay!
Each day is Valentine's day

Is your figure less than Greek?
Is your mouth a little weak?
When you open it to speak
Are you smart?

But don't change your hair for me
Not if you care for me
Stay little Valentine, stay!

Each day is Valentine's Day.[44]

****

I can hardly get over the impact on me of Woody Allen's 2011 film, *Midnight in Paris*. It is so hilariously evocative of the 1920s, and so

---

[44] Frank Sinatra, "My Funny Valentine"; Ascap.

vividly exemplifies the concept of conflict. Gil Pender, the protagonist, brilliantly downplayed by Owen Wilson, is engaged to the firmly Californian damsel, superficial Inez (Rachel MacAdams), but on his midnight forays into Paris's artistic past he falls in love with the fetching Adriana (Marion Cotillard), former mistress of Braque and Picasso. There are other sub-plots, but the main "character" is Paris in the rain; and the Cole Porter music of the era is totally apt and enchanting. In short, *Midnight in Paris* is easily Allen's best film since *Annie Hall,* if not his best, most mature, ever. Talk about "growing up puer"! … I think it deserved every Academy Award in the book; it was nominated for several, but won only Best Original Screenplay. When I first watched this movie, I immediately wanted to go and live in Paris. And I still do after my third viewing this New Year's Eve, 2012 moving into 2013.

Of course I am pretty much past it at this point, and I later lost my heart to Zurich anyway, but how vividly I recall living in Paris for six months in 1959. At the age of 23, just off the boat and sexually hungry, I happened to snare a multilinguist in a dance hall on the famed Champs Elyssées. Her name was Chantal. She camped out with me in a mirrored hotel room on the Left Bank until I ran out of travellers' checks. I don't blame Chantal for debouching, though I had come to love her. (Well, I was a pretty easy mark then when it came to falling in love, and still am.) Mostly I remember our strolls along the Seine, as depicted in this film, and the atmosphere of Paris that was so charming and exhilarating at the time. I actually wrote some of my best juvenilia in those few months, typing on an Olivetti, as if I were Hemingway or F. Scott Fitzgerald. (The psychological concept of "inflation" was not yet known to me.)

I honestly do think of going back to re-experience Paris, not with a typewriter in this day and age, but with my Mac Air. This is regression combined with technological progress. Of course, we know that without a lover, Paris is just another big city to feel lonely in. I mean no offence to singles, but I find it is not much fun going anywhere without a lover; and *with* one, it doesn't much matter where you go. To love is to be reborn every day into a new world. Not to love is to die a slow and boring death. It reflects ill of us to choose the latter. Just saying.

6
Badger Four:
THINK FOR YOURSELF

The Doing Syndrome

I mean to be piquante but not jejune. In the upper, human world, there is a *cultural imperative* to be productive, as in plant a garden, write a book, paint a picture, play the flute, knit a scarf, make babies, raise geese, sing a song and so on. It all derives from left-brain thinking. Don't just sit there like a toad in the hole, DO something. To where does this lead?—ambition, materialism, fame, fortune, fatigue, depression, even suicide. The drive to be productive collectively takes us away from immediate personal concerns, like relating to our partners, our children, our neighbors and ourselves. Some call it *multitasking*. But by whatever name, I think it is not good for society, and it does not bode well for our civilization, which everywhere flounders under the weight of religious and sectarian rulers who deny fundamental human rights to their citizens. Corruption is endemic, and donors to charitable causes know not where their money goes. Life itself is a lottery.

In Badgerland, life is passively simpler. We don't have to DO or MAKE anything. We don't have to PRODUCE anything or MULTI-TASK. We function in a right-brain way, imaginatively. We celebrate life by just BEING. We eat when we're hungry and make love when we feel loving. We play when we feel playful, and sleep when we're tired. We don't have to run about, always on the go, driving to a concert, jogging, doing yoga, lifting weights, swimming lengths, etc. In the upper world, humans HURRY, HURRY, HURRY. We saunter and mosey along, taking our time. Okay, we still have to forage for food and do the dishes and laundry, but they are done in the flow of everyday life, child's play compared to being productive. Of course, we may have a toke now and then, but where's the harm in that?

Now, there may be those who benefit psychologically from being hyperactive (e.g., so-called A-types), but perhaps they were held down by overly protective parents and are merely making up for lost time. But I will not belabor the obvious, and I also may be wrong. Suffice to say that many people are caught up in a hurly-burly life-style that is not their free choice.

Take, for instance, this book my patron Daemon is struggling to write. D. is fond of saying that he's not famous, merely prolific. And he is that. But the thing is, no one is waiting for another book by D. (this would be his 25th). He knows that, but he persists. This is beyond being productive; it is verging on the pathetic or pathological. I give up on D. In spite of his years in analysis, I am afraid he is certifiable. Well, what the hell, I don't mind, as long as he throws me some vegetables from time to time, and Bo Peep stays close.

Personally, I don't need to create or write anything in order to confirm my existence. Screw Descartes. I be, therefore I am, and that's enough for me. Make of it what you will.

Couples

I was just thinking of when I first got together with Bo Peep. We were so passionately attached to each other, we could not stand being apart for two minutes. When we weren't eating, we were watching a movie, holding hands or making love. Every day was badger heaven, and still is.

Of course we have tiffs from time to time, like any couple. They typically involve her sharp-tongued animus and my over-sensitive mother-bound anima. At least that's how D. sees it, and I, a Simple Simon, so to speak, can but agree. Well, we ain't Ozzie & Harriet. So sue me.

That calls for a tune by the Beatles:

> Let's all get up and dance to a song
> That was a hit before your mother was born
> Though she was born a long, long time ago
> Your mother should know (Your mother should ...)
> Your mother should know (...know)
> Sing it again
> Let's all get up and dance to a song
> That was a hit before your mother was born
> Though she was born a long, long time ago

Your mother should know (Your mother should ...)
Your mother should know (... know)

Lift up your hearts and sing me a song
That was a hit before your mother was born
Though she was born a long, long time ago
Your mother should know (Your mother should.)
Your mother should know (aaaaah)
Your mother should know (Your mother should.)
Your mother should know (aaaaah)

Sing it again
Da da da da.
Though she was born a long, long time ago
Your mother should know (Your mother should.)
Your mother should know (... know)
Your mother should know (Your mother should.)
Your mother should know (... know)
Your mother should know (Your mother should.)
Your mother should know. (... know)[45]

****

Of course, D. has his own perspective, and I don't begrudge him that. He thinks he's top dog, so to speak, and I let him wallow in that fantasy, because he would otherwise fall to pieces. Well, to each his own; love what you love, though I know that at least half his material comes from me.

Health and More

I am not generally hypochondriacal. I never fancy or invent vague illnesses (e.g., I don't suffer from 'Munchhausen by Proxy'). But I have this little lump beside my right eyebrow, and I am afraid it could be my spleen surfacing. Could that even be possible? Or perhaps the gods of evolution have chosen me to be the first badger unicorn. Or the first to have cancer of the forehead. I have tried to book an apt. with my epidemiologist, Dr. Balderdash, but alas he is not available until next March (i.e., 3 months away). So much for Canada's vaunted heath-care system.

---

[45] "Your Mother Should Know," on *Magical Mystery Tour*, music and lyrics by Lennon and McCartney; Ascap.

There is no one in the badger network to ask about this. We have no MSF (medicins sans frontiers) listening to us or even seeking us out. For shame, I say!

The volunteers called "doctors without borders" go to far-flung out-posts like Iceland and Surinam and Tonga, while we badgers have the highest rate of ear wax and toe jam in the known Western underworld. We need to band together—"Badgers without Borders"—an under-ground special ops brigade that brooks no nonsense, takes no prisoners, refuses any stipend. This would make badger history, and all little badgers proud if their poppas died in the line of duty.

****

Remember the mantra: "Don't write yourself out; leave something for the next day."

And then some.

Meanwhile, Happy Hanukah and Merry Christmas. Music streams in and out of my ears.

7
Daemon Three:
FARE THEE WELL, ANNABELLE

Four a.m. already. Heavens to Betsy, I used to be an early bird who got the worm, in bed at 10 and up at 7. Now I can't seem to get going until midnight, and then I'm an Eveready bunny.

What can I say? It is the writer's lot to keep odd hours thinking odd thoughts. Boris Pasternak had this to say about the craft:

> The writer is the Faust of modern society, the only surviving individual in a mass age. To his orthodox contemporaries he seems a semi-madman.[46]

More cheerfully, Ralph Waldo Emerson writes:

> The writer, like the priest, must be exempted from secular labor. His work needs a frolic health; he must be at the top of his condition.[47]

Well, amen to "frolic health"! But I am not beyond doubting myself, what I think or feel, and how I express it to others. This is endemic to the craft, whatever fuels late hours—pot, booze or a lover—no doubt about that. It's a slippery slope to lipstick and false eyelashes.

A writer is like a lizard drinking: one moment he is flat on the ground, and then he may suddenly bite your toes.

Not my fault. Just the messenger.

It was in such a depressive mood recently that, with some reluctance, I sent my half-finished manuscript for review (without my name on it) to a local respected editor, a Nurse-Ratchet-type who doesn't spare the rod and favors electro-shock. You see, I wanted to hear the worst, and I was not disappointed. Here is a brief taste of her summary execution:

> Utter rubbish. Not writing but typing. In my forty years in this business, I have never read such nonsense. And the badger metaphor, Bo Peep? I mean, talk about suspension of disbelief!? This writer should learn to do

---

[46] Jon Winokur, ed., *Writers on Writing,* p. 328
[47] Ibid., p. 333.

something useful, like market-gardening, locksmithing, canning tomatoes or welding.

Now, do I care? Well, yes, I wept, I lost sleep, for I can be hurt by the opinions of others. But let them suck eggs, for as it happens I have my own publishing house, so I can publish whatever I bloody well want, however whimsical or execrable. This automatically trumps the opinions of a bevy of Ms. Ratchets. Of course my manuscript isn't *War and Peace* or *Moby-Dick*, but it is mine own, and I have no peer in the genre of Jungian romance, a fact Ms. Ratchet ignored in her killer critique.

It is 6 a.m. now, and I must to bed shortly. But I have enjoyed the solitude in which I could write unfettered. This is a situation not easily wrought in anyone's hurly-burly day. I am grateful for my peaceful life, lonely as it sometimes feels.

I am ready to leave my computer now, but one more tidbit before I go, brought to my attention by the Antipodean woman I call my sweetheart, who just happens to resemble Badger's description of Bo Peep.

Reverse Ferrets

There is lately (Fall, 2012) a brouhaha over a stupid prank that may have contributed to, or even caused, the suicide of a nurse in England. Two radio DJs in Australia, seeking an interview with Princess Kate Middleton, called the hospital where she was recuperating. An Aussie journalist,[48] concerned that the Australian regulatory body has overreacted to this particular case and now contemplates stiff regulations on the press to curb such activities in the future, writes:

> Community reaction to [Australian radio DJs] Greig and Christian is partly driven by displaced anger at the unwillingness of the broadcaster and the inability of the broadcasting regulator to deal appropriately with a far worse offender [presumably media personality Kyle Sandilands], who has flouted basic expectations of decency with apparent impunity because of his capacity to generate revenue.

---

[48] Canberra correspondent Bernard Keane on resisting the witch hunt over the royal prank call in October 2012 (from *Crikey*, Independent media, 10 December, 2012).

Money, free speech and community reactions are all pulling the issue in different directions. The reaction of both the UK and local media is driven by the need to monetise the story, and if exploiting it means the likes of the *Daily Mail* turning on a penny, that's fine: **reverse all the ferrets**.[49]

But the tragedy also touched that deep-seated Australian instinct to regulate away unpopular things. The ultimate logic of much of the anger directed towards the broadcaster is that nothing that causes offence to anyone anywhere should be broadcast, because there's always a possibility that someone will react in a tragic way, even if that couldn't have been reasonably foreseen by a broadcaster.

So here I am, defending the right of a broadcasting licensee I loathe to make a poorly executed prank call that seems to have caused a heartbreaking outcome. Still, none of the alternatives—the baying for blood of the hypocrites of the British tabloids, the imperial mentality of a discredited police force, or the impulse to further restrict speech based on unforeseeable consequences—strike me as preferable.

Oh pshaw, pshaw! The Australian government, and every other, had better turn their attention to the packaging of everyday products—you can hardly get into a box of cereal or a jar of peanut butter without a pair of pliers or a wrench, and medicines?—forget about it; one could die in the attempt; since a lone maniac in the 1970s tampered with a bottle of Tylenol, everything from Vitamin D to mouthwash is sealed tighter than the Straits of Gibraltar. Seniors beware.

And while I'm on a rant, how about a toothpaste dispenser that uses it all, instead of the hapless tubes that just fizzle out, however tightly squeezed, and clutter up our landfill sites?

---

[49] The British media typically use this term to describe a sudden volte-face in a newspaper's editorial line on a certain issue. Generally this will involve no acknowledgment of the previous position. The term originates from Kelvin MacKenzie's time [as editor] at [the British tabloid] *The Sun*. His preferred description of the role of journalists when it came to public figures was to "stick a ferret up their trousers". This meant making their lives uncomfortable, based on the northern [English] so-called sport of ferret-legging (where contestants compete to show who can endure a live ferret within their sealed trousers the longest). However, when it became clear that the tide of public opinion had turned against the paper's line, MacKenzie would burst from his office shouting **"Reverse Ferret!"** – From *Wikipedia* (modified).

****

On a lighter note, I do deplore the timekeeping move from analogue to digital. I have half a dozen wristwatches, all analogue. I have a bedside alarm clock, digital, and it is such a pain to go around the clock to reset it for an earlier time. Now I ask you: they put a man on the moon; why can't they make digital clocks that you can wind backward? It's a small issue in the grand scheme of things, but it does make me crazy. Again, in my psychological trade, this is called being complexed—as we all are by someone or something...

****

More than jazz

The great pianist Dave Brubeck died this week at the age of 92. He was a phenomenon. He had a long and fruitful life. His improvisational style and collaboration with saxophonist Paul Desmond changed the world of jazz, notably with "Take Five." I never saw him live, but I was privileged to grow up hearing his fantastic compositions and improvisations that historically (1959-64) put an end to bebop. We all mourn an innovative, improvisational genius, a master musician who more or less invented what came to be called cool jazz. Controversial at the time, Brubeck's approach to jazz has over the years become the gold standard. His playing has been called complexity combined with simplicity. He sold a gazillion records, appeared on *Time* magazine's cover in 1964, and made jazz "popular"; well, at least acceptable to the mainstream. He remains one of my heroes who individuated by following his personal star. Dave Brubeck was and still is hot and cool at the same time; call it groovy, and that bin a hard act to follow.[50]

I could also write a tribute to jazz-men Charlie Parker and John Coltrane, but that's for another book, if ever.

****

---

[50] I write this listening to "Fare Thee Well, Annabelle," on the album *Jazz, Red Hot and Cool;* Ascap.

Bacteria

They are everywhere, pesky little devils—on clothes, bodies and furniture. There is no way to avoid germs, even with Lysol. They sometimes manifest as influenza. Now, I have felt wretched all week with stomach flu, voiding at both ends. I saw my Doctor Sophia yesterday and she recommended *arsenicum album*. This is a homeopathic remedy for stomach and bowels in an uproar. Of course, you know the back story of homeopathy—"like cures like," in small doses. Well, it seems to be working.

Undiluted arsenic is known to be fatal, and said to be the poison of choice over the years by female killers. However, as it happens, there lurks in the stomach and bowels an arsenic-like amoeba, namely *arsenicum album,* that can get out of control, go rogue, according to homeopathic theory (Google it). Now, *acidophilus* has no such pedigree, but you can still Google it for the full story, which is scary but not all bad, for it does settle the gut.

Now, while I am taking this diarrhea inhibitive, I am also taking a mild laxative, *Psyllium.* Talk about the opposites; playing both ends against the middle, so to speak. Just saying ...

****

Now it is past dawn and I have entered the liminal, morass zone that many writers know—whether to go to bed or keep stewing over words. I often choose to stick with it—rock around the clock, as it were—but this morning I will choose the arms of Morpheus, ancient god of sleep. And besides, I have developed a hurtful blister on my palm from using the computer mouse.

> Good night,
> Sleep tight,
> Don't let the bedbugs bite.

But before I go, the following is so rich that it deserves wide dissemination among the cognoscenti and literati who favor those faddish but fiendish eBook readers like Kindle, Android and iPad.

It is on a bookmark given out to customers by a Toronto bookseller:

Technological Breakthrough!

Introducing the new *Bio-Optic Organized Knowledge* device—

BOOK

BOOK is a revolutionary breakthrough in technology; no wires, no electric circuits, no batteries, no buttons, nothing to be connected or switched on. *It's easy to use. Even a child can operate it.*

Compact and portable, it can be used anywhere—in bed or sitting in an armchair —yet powerful enough to hold as much as a CD-ROM.

BOOK is constructed of sequentially numbered sheets of paper (recyclable), each capable of holding thousands of bits of information. The pages are locked together with one of two different custom devices, a BINDER, or DOUBLE STITCH BINDING, which keep the sheets in their correct sequence. Opaque Paper Technology (OPT) allows manufacturers to use both sides of the sheet, doubling the information density.

Each sheet is scanned optically, registering information directly to your brain. A flick of the finger takes you to the next sheet.

BOOK never crashes or requires rebooting. The "browse" feature allows instant movement to any sheet, forward or backward, to where one wishes. Many come with an "index" feature, which pinpoints the exact location of any selected information for instant retrieval.

Portable, durable and affordable, BOOK is being hailed as a precursor of a new entertainment wave. BOOK's appeal seems so certain that thousands of content creators have committed to the platform and investors are reportedly flocking to the medium. Look for a flood of new BOOKS at …

BOOK CITY

Now, isn't that delightful? Personally, I see the importance of BOOKS as comparable historically to the invention of the wheel, and of course they owe much to the pioneering genius of Johannes Gutenberg (c. 1398–1468). I therefore predict that BOOKS will displace electronic versions of the written word within the next 3 to 5 years. I know that readers of Inner City titles do prefer printed pages to bytes of information from the ether that might have had dozens of partners before (possibly carrying a virus).

8
Razr Has a Ball
EROS = SOPHIA BECOMNG

* Now, Emma Lou.
It was twilight, loneliest time of day.
I almost tripped over her
as she was panhandling in Toronto
on the corner of Queen Street West and John.
She was playing a juice (Jew's) harp, not too badly.
It's a very trendy area,
and her cup was already half full with bills and coins.
She was waifish, disheveled, hiding behind a cowboy hat.
I liked her at once, thanks to my savior complex.
Well, I am a real sucker for anyone
who reminds me of Mimi in *La Bohème.*
I knelt down. "Hey there, little lady, what's your name?"
"Emma Lou," she shrugged. "Who wants to know?"
"I'm Razr," I said, choosing my usual *nom de guerre.*
"I have a mini-mansion in Rosedale. I could give you shelter."
"You won't hurt me, mister, will you?" she asked.
"No chance," I replied.
I helped Emma Lou to her feet.
She gathered up her few things and the money basket
and I popped her into my harvest gold VW (GTI/VR6).

I first took Emma Lou to my house,
perhaps to show her that I was a man of means
 and meant no harm.
I don't know if she knew
that Rosedale is a pretty pricey area of Toronto.
It wasn't when I bought my house here
Thirty years ago.
Now the prices are out of sight.
Anyway, Emma Lou seemed impressed by the oak staircases
and artwork and kissed me heartily.

Eros = Sophia Becoming

"Thank you," she breathed, "you are a good man."
Well, we'd see about that later,
for I was already thinking
of tearing her clothes off.
Then, after touring my house,
I steered Emma Lou to my favorite local Thai restaurant.
We feasted and walked back to my house hand in hand.
I do like that feeling of intimacy.
At home, I filled up my tiny new 4-cup
Betty Crocker coffee machine.
We were quiet, sipping decaf and Cointreau.
I did not press her for the circumstances
that found her on the street.
Well, I may have a savior complex,
but I'm not the Grand Inquisitor or the angel Gabriel.

"It's bin a long day," said Emma Lou finally, "I bin so tired."
"Yes, my dear," I said. "Come, I will care for you."

I led Emma Lou to the ensuiteheart on the third floor,
where I tucked her in under the duvet and kissed her chastely.
"Sweet dreams," I said, "I will come at your call."
"Please don't leave," she said, "I bin so lonely."
Well, I am a gentleman, first and last.
I put on a CD of Billie Holiday, undressed, pulled back the covers,
and settled in beside Emma Lou.
"You smell so good, like jasmine and cocoa butter," I whispered,
"and you saved me from jumping offa bridge."
"Me too, you silly," she said, and then,
"Are you into foreplay?" she asked shyly.
"You bet," I replied, "until the cows come home."
And so we did until falling asleep at dawn.

This seemed to suit us both,
and before I knew it the alarm was buzzing,
for I had a client at 9 a.m.
We made love thereafter occasionally,
but not seriously.

In her thirties, Emma Lou married an acrobat

85

in the Cirque du Soleil
and bore him adorable twin girls,
Gabriella and Sophia.

****

There once was an older woman
who passed by my house
from time to time. (By older
I mean more or less my own age,
no spring chicken.)
Anyway, one day she saw me struggling
up the porch steps with a bag of groceries
in one hand, a cane in the other,
and she rushed over to help me.
That's how we met.

I was grateful and invited her in
for coffee or wine and a chat.
I had no intention
of molesting her, nor did I that.
We relaxed in the leather chairs
in which I sit opposite a client
delving into the unconscious. But
I did not ask if she dreamed.

"My name is Natalie," she said shyly.
I was immediately taken back in time.
I said, "Do you remember Bob & Ray,
A comedy team in the 1960s?"
"No," she giggled.
"Well," I observed, "they had
an imaginary girl friend they called
Natalie Attired. Always broke me up."

She was crying.
"Oh, I bin so lonely," she said.

We remain
passing friends to this very day,
and Eros reigns supreme.

Eros = Sophia Becoming

****

I am in Negril Village at the notorious half-nudist
Hedonism II resort in Jamaica.
I chose this all-inclusive vacation
as compensation for my lonely, introverted turret.
It lives up to its reputation.
On the beach I am surrounded by naked women.
I would like to hook up with one,
but they are mostly under thirty and unlikely
to be interested in a balding old snort like me,
nor I in them.
I browse the beach for mature women
close to my own age,
and wonder how on earth to approach one.

"Hi there, Susan Sarandon looks a lot like you."
"Cameron Diaz has your legs."
"Hi there, love your outfit. What's your name?
Can I buy you a free drink?"
"Pardon me, may I join you, or is this sand taken?"

My incipient erection slowly abates and I lie down on a beach towel.
I fall into a dreamy state until I feel a touch on my shoulder.
I open my eyes to see a lovely naked lady plop down beside me.
"I saw you checking us out," she says. "I was sorry you passed me by."
"And why is that?" I asked.
"Most men here are jocks," she said, "little boys looking to get drunk
and laid.
"I'm worth more than that, and you look like my kind of guy."
"Well said," I opine. "But I too would like to make love."
"All in good time, my friend," she laughs. "Let's have a drink.
"I am Piper. Make mine rum and coke."
"Razr here, at your service," I say,
I trek to the closest nude swim-up bar and pick up drinks.
Mine is Johnny Walker Black Label choked with ice.
It is noon and my first drink of the day.
Piper is lying on her back.
Nothing on but Hugo Boss sunglasses.

Toned body for a woman her age—
more or less fifty, I guess, but I can't tell anymore.
Blonde hair turning white, but complexion right out of l'Oréal—
a zoomer, as they're called these days—Boomer with zip.
She sits up and sips her drink.
"I want you to know," she says,
"that I am employed by this resort
to make our guests feel welcome and comfortable,
so they will come back again.
But still, I am free to choose my companions.
Today I have chosen you.
And if it comes to making consensual love,
that is part of the welcome wagon."
She pauses.
"Personally, I long for an experienced, mature man
to explore my mind and body, to appreciate me as I am,
not his projected image of me."
I sit with Piper for about an hour. We apply sun-tan lotion
to each other and talk of books and psychology and sealing wax.
"Piper," I finally say, "you're my kind of girl. Come with me."
We pick up our towels and walk hand in hand to my room overlooking
giant gardenias and eucalyptus. I mean, it feels like Paradise.
I help Piper onto the bed and say, "Let's take our time. You are so
beautiful, how do you stand it?"
She smiles. "I avoid mirrors."
I would like to disrobe Piper, but she is already naked
(the downside of being a nudist).
I lie beside her and caress her tanned body.
She takes hold of me and gentles me into shape.
"I fall in love too easily," I whisper, thinking of Chet Baker.
We frolicked until dawn, occasionally talking of Rilke,
Carl Jung, Paul Tillich, Dave Brubeck,
and the mysteries of love.
She is clearly of my generation and no dummy.
"You are a gentle man, Mr. Razr,"
Piper says as she flits out the door in the morning
after a shower.

"That was special fun.

"Sorry to leave, but I have an early shift today."

"See you on the beach," I waved.

****

One of the things about casual sex is that it's never as casual as you intend or pretend it to be at the time. The intimacy with another may linger on long after the coupling. You are captivated by Eros, naturally.

And so the next day I scoured the beach for a glimpse of Piper, in hopes of furthering our connection, but I saw her not. Well, nothing strange about that. She was a hired gun, after all, and she had a job to do that only whimsically and temporarily included me.

I could live with that, but not easily. I really liked Piper, and I could have loved her. Silly me, so vulnerable to Eros and the animal in me.

A little later, off the beach, I began thinking about how technology has outpaced our capacity to deal with it, let alone understand what is behind it, how it works. Take, for instance, a modern cellphone, It is barely a handed years since Alexander Graham Bell sent a feeble signal across the Atlantic and now we have a spider-like communications network of underground and overground cables—not to mention the millions of invisible wi-fi waves that only a few dedicated worker bees understand and know how to use. I could say the same about the electrical lines that invade your house and make lighting possible and power your computer. What makes modern life possible is all a mystery to most of us. And talk about plumbing! Do you know why and how your toilet flushes? The magic that goes into having a hot shower?

There will yet come a reckoning, the shadow side of everything we take for granted today. Global climate change will bring us to our knees, seeking solace from, what or whom? a Supreme Being? Scientists?

All that is conjecture. Sorry, no answers, I'm just the messenger.

****

By now, and especially if you have read Master Daemon's previous books, you will realize that I am his lascivious alter-ego, repressed but never forgotten—in a Jungian sense, not, God forbid, in Freud's terms. Indeed, D. welcomes me into his life when appropriate, and I respond as if I were Robin answering Batman's call for assistance, or Tonto by the side of the Lone Ranger, Kemo Sabe.

I don't really know where Badger fits in to D.'s psychic life but I trust it will become clear in time. Badger has been underground for so long, who can fathom it? Never mind, he is no threat to me, for as an alternate personality I have D. by the knackers and he knows it.

Now, in case you are confused about whether Bo Peep is a badger or a human woman, I can assure you she is the latter, shy but forthcoming. You see, I have hands-on knowledge of the winsome Bo Peep (if I may be so bold as to say), and I do what I can to facilitate her further coupling with Daemon. He loves her like elephant—which means fiercely, with lasting fidelity. And as far as I can tell, she feels the same. This is not easy to discern from where I generally stand—in the shadow. I am not the fabled Phantom of the Opera, after all, or a Flying Dutchman, just a pale substitute for those iconic figures.

Well, that's what I do and why I'm here. So let's see what's going on in Daemon's unconscious, for that is the voice of truth, trumping anything Badger or I could say about his love-life. For a start, here is one of his most recent dreams:

****

I am in a dance hall. Very exclusive club, invitation only. Some are masked, many are naked. Some are copulating, and there are a few threesomes apparently having a fine time. I don't know what to do, but a pretty young lass with not a stitch on takes my hand and leads me to a sofa, a SETTee, if you will. There she proceeds to lovingly disrobe me and coax me into making love. I don't feel like a victim.

The scene changes. Now I am part of a foursome. It is hard for me to get my head around what position to assume, but a big black man guides me into a labial treasure.

I wake up happily, though perplexed.

****

I will not judge Daemon, for that is not my mandate. But I think it is clear that this dream can be understood in the context of what D. himself has noted—*pudendum absconditum*. I mean to say the obvious: D. has not had a woman in his bed since he frolicked with his true sweetheart Bo Peep some three years ago now. His unconscious compensates by putting him into erotic situations that consciously he would never countenance.

After such a dream, however, D. might be alert to the possibilities of Eros, naturally, in his daily life.

Just saying ... but I have the same analytic training as D., though I live in a supposedly darker place.

Now, D. has acknowledged his aloneness in his turret. So far, so good. But why doesn't he do something about it? He may claim to be waiting faithfully for Bo Peep, but for how long can he sustain this hope, or fantasy? And just here we enter the zone of the unknown.

Think seriously about the homeopathic mantra, "like cures like," and how it might apply to Master Daemon's situation. To me, it implies that an erotic adventure or two would not go amiss in D.'s life.

Very well. I am much too tired now to pursue this line of thought, but I expect you get my drift. Badger's Bo Peep had it right: "You're only old once, so enjoy it." And after all, I'm only the Greek chorus, so to speak.

****

Bo Peep stirred and wagged her head at Razr, "He's retarded, right?"

"Keep your fur on, sweetheart," I said, "he is just age-appropriate libidinous."

9
Daemon Four:
LAST MAN STANDING

1 will admit it—I do like Razr. His erotic propensities and adventures into the erogenous zone compensate my chaste turret life.

Not what you expected? Well, me either. Which reminds me of my analyst's mantra: "Expect the unexpected; life is boring without it."

I am not officially vegetarian, as some of my children are (eating nothing that flies, walks, swims or quacks), but all the same I don't eat much meat any more. Just lost my taste for it. Instead, I survive on eggs and noodles, root-vegetable soups, corn flakes, fish fillets, tofu salads, bananas, peanut butter and fresh berries. About once a month I might have a guilty hamburger.

In case you can't read the small print in the above ad, here it is:

How soon is too soon? Not soon enough. Laboratory tests over the last few years have proven that babies who start drinking soda during that early formative period have a much higher chance of gaining acceptance and "fitting in" during those awkward pre-teen and teen years. So do yourself a favor. Do your child a favor. Start them on a strict regimen of sodas and other sugary carbonated beverages right now, for a lifetime of guaranteed happiness.[51]

And bad teeth! Now I ask you, is there no end to the idiocy the Western world has not, or will not, stoop to, to make a buck? Capitalism ...

I am far from being a communist, but there sure is a lot about our Western system that irks me. I could talk about the environment, the high cost of dental work, natural gas pipelines to New Brunswick and the lack of day-care spaces, but that would take us much too far afield. Let's just say I have a lot in common with Badger.

****

I once said to Rebecca, "Give me a sentence and I'll write three pages." Well, now I've written over 90, and I have had the biscuit.

So, see you later, à bientôt in French, or as they say in Zurich, bis später; or in Beijing, chow mein.

> One two three four five six seven,
> All good children go to Heaven.[52]

If this turns out to be the first book of something called *The Badger Trilogy,* be kind. It's endemic to my writing complex.

So let me leave you with another catchy tune by the Beatles:

> When I wake up early in the morning,
> Lift my head, I'm still yawning.
> When I'm in the middle of a dream,
> Stay in bed float up stream.
> Please don't wake me, no don't shake me,

---

[51] From the archives of *The Soda Pop Board of America,* ca. 1923.
[52] From the Beatles, "You Never Give Me Your Money"; Ascap.

Leave me where I am, I'm only sleeping.
Everybody seems to think I'm lazy. I don't mind,
I think they're crazy.
Running everywhere at such a speed.
Till they find, there's no need.
Please don't spoil my day, I'm on my way.
And after all, I'm only sleeping.

Keeping an eye on the world going by my window,
Taking my time, lying there and staring at the ceiling,
Waiting for the sleepy feeling.
Please don't spoil my day, I'm miles away.
And after all, I'm only sleeping.

Keeping an eye on the world going by my window.
Taking my time, when I wake up early in the morning,
Lift my head, I'm still yawning.
When I'm in the middle of a dream, stay in bed,
floating up stream.
Please don't wake me, no don't shake me,
leave me where I am
I'm only sleeping.[53]

Now, again it is 3 a.m., and I will join Bo Peep in bed at last. Well, who wouldn't? And I hope you've had fun too.

---

[53] "I'm Only Sleeping," on *Revolver,* lyrics by John Lennon; Ascap.

JUNG AND RESTLESS

10
Badger Five:
POINT, SETT, MATCH

D. may be the last man standing, but I get the last word. So much for the fickle finger of fate, or call it irony.

I am glad to be let back into this book, for although I eschew the upper world, I do not disdain it. I esteem my patron D. for his hard work in making available the ideas and application of the works of Dr. Jung, so long as he doesn't forget us animals who underpin, and may sometimes undermine, his rational left-brain intentions.

Just saying, and here is Dr. Jung himself to make the point

> Eros is a questionable fellow and will always remain so whatever the legislation of the future may have to say about it. He belongs on one side to man's primordial animal nature which will endure as long as man has an animal body. On the other side he is related to the highest forms of the spirit. But he thrives only when spirit and instinct are in right harmony. If one or the other aspect is lacking to him the result is injury or at least a lopsidedness that may easily veer toward the pathological. Too much of the animal distorts the civilized man, too much civilization makes sick animals. This dilemma reveals the vast uncertainty that Eros holds for man.
>
> "Eros is a mighty daemon," as the wise Diotima said to Socrates. We shall never get the better of him, or only to our own hurt.[54]

And so I rest my case, with a final note from the Grand Master:

> Nonsense streams from the deepest wells, amply like the Nile.[55]

---

[54] "Two Essays," CW 7, pars. 32f.
[55] Jung, *The Red Book,* p. 336, col. 2 (with thanks to J. Gary Sparks).

BIBLIOGRAPHY
(with recommended reading)

Carotenuto, Aldo. *Eros and Pathos: Shades of Love and Suffering.* Toronto: Inner City Books, 1989.

Cohen, Leonard. *Book of Longing.* Toronto: McClelland & Stewart Ltd., 2006.

Daumal, René. *Mount Analogue: An Authentic Narrative.* Trans. and Intro. Robert Shattuck. London, UK: Vincent Stuart Publishers Ltd., 1959.

De Vries, Ad. *Dictionary of Symbols and Imagery.* Amsterdam: North-Holland Publishing Company, 1976.

Edinger, Edward F. *Anatomy of the Psyche: Alchemical Symbolism in Psychotherapy.* La Salle, IL: Open Court, 1985.

_____. *The Creation of Consciousness: Jung's Myth for Modern Man.* Toronto: Inner City Books, 1984.

_____. "M. Esther Harding, 1888-1971." In *Spring 1972.* Zurich: Spring Publications, 1972.

_____. *The Mysterium Lectures: A Journey Through Jung's* Mysterium Coniunctionis. Toronto: Inner City Books, 1995.

_____. *The Mystery of the Coniunctio: Alchemical Image of Individuation.* Toronto: Inner City Books, 1994.

_____. *Transformation of the God-Image: An Elucidation of Jung's* Answer to Job. Toronto: Inner City Books, 1992.

_____. *Science of the Soul: A Jungian Perspective.* Toronto: Inner City Books, 2002.

Elder, George R., and Cordic, Dianne D., eds. *An American Jungian: In Honor of Edward F. Edinger.* Toronto: Inner City Books, 2009.

Eliot, T. S. *Four Quartets.* London, UK: Faber and Faber Limited, 1959.

Emerson, Ralph Waldo. *Essays: First and Second Series.* Intr. Douglas Crase. New York: Penguin Books (Library of America), 2010.

_____. *Selected Journals, 1841-1877.* New York: Penguin Books (Library of America), 2010.

Bibliography

Frey-Rohn, Liliane. *From Freud to Jung: A Comparative Study of the Psychology of the Unconscious.* Boston: Shambhala Publications, 1974.

Frost, Robert. "Stopping by Woods on a Snowy Evening." In "The Poetry of Robert Frost," Ed. Edward Connery Lathem, from *The Random House Book of Poetry for Children.* New York: Random House, 1983.

Grimm Brothers. *The Complete Grimm's Fairy Tales.* New York: Pantheon Books, 1944.

Hall, James A., and Sharp, Daryl, eds. *Marie-Louise von Franz: The Classic Jungian and the Classic Jungian Tradition.* Toronto: Inner City Books, 2008.

Hannah, Barbara. *Jung: His Life and Work (A Biographical Memoir).* New York: Capricorn Books, G.P. Putnam's Sons, 1976.

Hollis, James. *The Middle Passage: From Misery to Meaning in Midlife.* Toronto: Inner City Books, 1993.

_____. *The Eden Project: In Search of the Magical Other.* Toronto: Inner City Books, 1998.

_____. *Under Saturn's Shadow: The Wounding and Healing of Men.* Toronto: Inner City Books, 1994.

Jacoby, Mario. *The Analytic Encounter: Transference and Human Relationship.* Toronto: Inner City Books, 1984.

_____. *Longing for Paradise: Psychological Perspectives on an Archetype.* Toronto: Inner City Books, 2006.

Jung, C. G. *C. G. Jung Letters.* (Bollingen Series XCV). 2 vols. Ed. G. Adler and A. Jaffé. Princeton: Princeton University Press, 1973.

_____. *The Collected Works of C. G. Jung* (Bollingen Series XX). 20 vols. Trans. R. F. C. Hull. Ed. H. Read, M. Fordham, G. Adler, Wm. McGuire. Princeton: Princeton University Press, 1953-1979.

_____. *Memories, Dreams, Reflections.* Ed. Aniela Jaffé. New York: Pantheon Books, 1961.

_____. *The Psychology of Kundalini Yoga: Notes of the Seminar Given in 1932 by C.G. Jung* (Bollingen Series XCIX). Ed. Sonu Shamdasani. Princeton: Princeton University Press, 1996.

_____. *Visions: Notes of the Seminar Given in 1930-1934* (Bollingen Series XCIX). 2 vols. Ed. Claire Douglas. Princeton: Princeton Univ. Press, 1997.

Jung, Carl G., and von Franz, Marie-Louise, eds. *Man and His Symbols*. London, UK: Aldus Books, 1964.

Kafka, Franz. [D1] *The Diaries of Franz Kafka, 1910-1913*. Trans. Joseph Kresh. Ed. Max Brod. London: Secker & Warburg, 1948.

_____. [D2] *The Diaries of Franz Kafka, 1914-1923*. Trans. Martin Greenberg. Ed. Max Brod. London: Secker & Warburg, 1949.

_____. *The Great Wall of China and Other Pieces*. Trans. Willa and Edwin Muir. London: Secker & Warburg, 1946.

Kaufmann, Walter, ed. and trans. *The Portable Nietzsche*. New York: Viking Press, 1954.

Kierkegaard, Søren. *The Journals of Kierkegaard: 1834-1854*. Ed. and trans. Alexander Dru. Oxford, UK: Oxford University Press, 1958.

Luton, Frith. *Bees, Honey and the Hive: Circumambulating the Centre (A Jungian Exploration of the Symbolism and Psychology)*. Toronto: Inner City Books, 2011.

Malcolm, Janet. *Psychoanalysis: The Impossible Profession*. New York: Alfred A. Knopf, 1981.

McGuire, William, ed. *The Freud/Jung Letters* (Bollingen Series XCIV). Trans. Ralph Manheim and R. F. C. Hull. Princeton: Princeton University Press, 1974.

McGuire, William, and Hull, R. F. C., eds. *C. G. Jung Speaking: Interviews and Encounters* (Bollingen Series XCVII). Princeton: Princeton University Press, 1977.

Meredith, Margaret Eileen. *The Secret Garden: Temenos for Individuation*. Toronto: Inner City Books, 2005.

Miller, Henry. *The Wisdom of the Heart*. New York: New Directions, 1950.

Monick, Eugene. *Phallos: Sacred Image of the Masculine*. Toronto: Inner City Books, 1987.

Perera, Sylvia Brinton. *Descent to the Goddess: A Way of Initiation for Women*. Toronto: Inner City Books, 1981.

_____. *The Scapegoat Complex: Toward a Mythology of Shadow and Guilt*. Toronto: Inner City Books, 1986.

Plato. *The Dialogues of Plato*. New York: Random House, 1965.

Bibliography

Qualls-Corbett, Nancy. *The Sacred Prostitute: Eternal Aspect of the Feminine.* Toronto: Inner City Books, 1988.

Rank, Otto. *The Trauma of Birth.* New York: Brunner, 1952.

Rilke, Rainer Maria. *The Notebook of Malte Laurids Brigge.* Trans. John Linton. London, UK: The Hogarth Press, 1959.

_____. *Rilke on Love and Other Difficulties.* Ed. John Mood. New York, Norton, 1975.

_____. *Rainer Maria Rilke, Sonnets to Orpheus.* Trans. Willis Barnstone. Boston, MA: Shambhala, 2004.

Sharp, Daryl. *The Brillig Trilogy.* See below: *Chicken Little; Who Am I, Really?;* and *Living Jung.*

_____. *Chicken Little: The Inside Story (a Jungian romance).* Toronto: Inner City Books, 1993.

_____. *C. G. Jung Lexicon: A Primer of Terms and Concepts.* Toronto: Inner City Books, 1991.

_____. *Dear Gladys: The Survival Papers, Book 2.* Toronto: Inner City Books, 1989.

_____. *Digesting Jung: Food for the Journey.* Toronto: Inner City Books, 2001.

_____. *The Eros Trilogy.* See *Live Your Nonsense; Trampled to Death by Gees;,* and *Hijacked by Eros.*

_____. *Eyes Wide Open: Late Thoughts (a Jungian romance).* Toronto: Inner City Books, 2007.

_____. *Getting To Know You: The Inside Out of Relationship.* Toronto: Inner City Books, 1992.

_____. *Jung Uncorked: Rare Vintages from the Cellar of Analytical Psychology.* 4 vols. Toronto: Inner City Books, 2008-9.

_____. *Jungian Psychology Unplugged: My Life as an Elephant.* Toronto, Inner City Books, 1998.

_____. *Live Your Nonsense: Halfway to Dawn with Eros (A Jungian Perspective on Individuation).* Toronto: Inner City Books, 2010.

_____. *Living Jung: The Good and the Better.* Toronto: Inner City Books, 1966.

_____. *Miles To Go Before I Sleep: Growing Up Puer (another Jungian romance).* Toronto: Inner City Books, 2013.

_____. *Not the Big Sleep: On Having Fun, Seriously (a Jungian romance).* Toronto: Inner City Books, 2005.

_____. *On Staying Awake: Getting Older and Bolder (another Jungian romance).* Toronto: Inner City Books, 2006.

_____. *Personality Types: Jung's Model of Typology.* Toronto: Inner City Books, 1987.

_____. *The Secret Raven: Conflict and Transformation in the Life of Franz Kafka.* Toronto: Inner City Books, 1980.

_____. *The SleepNot Trilogy.* See *Not the Big Sleep; On Staying Awake; and Eyes Wide Open.*

_____. *The Survival Papers: Anatomy of a Midlife Crisis.* Toronto: Inner City Books, 1988.

_____. *Trampled to Death by Geese: More Eros, and a Lot More Nonsense (A Jungian analyst's whimsical perspective on the Inner Life).* Toronto: Inner City Books, 2011.

_____. *Who Am I, Really? Personality, Soul and Individuation.* Toronto: Inner City Books, 1995.

Sparks, J. Gary. *At the Heart of Matter: Synchronicity and Jung's Spiritual Testament.* Toronto: Inner City Books, 2007.

_____. *In the Valley of Diamonds: Adventures in* Number and Time *with Marie-Louise von Franz.* Toronto: Inner City Books, 2009.

Stein, Gertrude. *Geography and Plays.* New York: Random House, 1922.

Stevens, Anthony. *Archetype Revisited: An Updated Natural History of the Self.* Toronto: Inner City Books, 2003.

_____. *The Talking Cure: Psychotherapy, Past, Present and Future.* 3 vols. Toronto: Inner City Books, 2013.

Storr, Anthony. *Solitude.* London, UK: HarperCollins Publishers, 1997.

Bibliography

Truss, Lynne. *Talk to the Hand: #?*! The Utter Bloody Rudeness of the World Today, or Six Good Reasons to Stay Home and Bolt the Door.* New York: Gotham Books (Penguin), 2005.

Von Franz, Marie-Louise. *Alchemy: An Introduction to the Symbolism and the Psychology.* Toronto: Inner City Books, 1980.

_____. *Animus and Anima in Fairy Tales.* Toronto: Inner City Books, 2002.

_____. *Archetypal Dimensions of the Psyche.* Boston: Shambhala Publications, 1997.

_____. *C. G. Jung: His Myth in Our Time.* Toronto: Inner City Books, 1998.

_____. *Individuation in Fairy Tales.* Zurich: Spring Publications, 1977.

_____. *On Divination and Synchronicity.* Toronto: Inner City Books, 1980.

_____. *The Problem of the Puer Aeternus.* Revised edition. Ed. Daryl Sharp. Toronto: Inner City Books, 2000.

_____. *Projection and Re-Collection in Jungian Psychology: Reflections of the Soul.* Trans. William H. Kennedy. La Salle, IL: Open Court, 1980.

_____. *Redemption Motifs in Fairy Tales.* Toronto: Inner City Books, 1980.

Von Franz, Marie-Louise, and Hillman, James. *Jung's Typology.* New York: Spring Publications, 1971.

Wilhelm, Richard, trans. *The I Ching or Book of Changes.* Rendered into English by Cary F. Baynes. London, UK: Routledge & Kegan Paul, 1968.

Winnicott, Donald.W. *Playing and Reality* London, UK: Penguin Books, 1991.

Winokur, Jon, ed. *W.O.W.: Writers on Writing.* Philadelphia, PA: Running Press, 1990.

Yeoman, Ann. *Now or Neverland: Peter Pan and the Myth of Eternal Youth.* Toronto: Inner City Books, 1999.

Index

Also by Daryl Sharp in this Series

Please see next page for discounts and postage/handling.

THE SECRET RAVEN: Conflict and Transformation in the Life of Franz Kafka
ISBN 978-0-919123-00-7. (1980) 128 pp. $25

PERSONALITY TYPES: Jung's Model of Typology
ISBN 978-0-919123-30-9. (1987) 128 pp. **Diagrams** $25

THE SURVIVAL PAPERS: Anatomy of a Midlife Crisis
ISBN 978-0-919123-34-2. (1988) 160 pp. $25

DEAR GLADYS: The Survival Papers, Book 2
ISBN 978-0-919123-36-6. (1989) 144 pp. $25

JUNG LEXICON: A Primer of Terms and Concepts
ISBN 978-0-919123-48-9. (1991) 160 pp. **Diagrams** $25

GETTING TO KNOW YOU: The Inside Out of Relationship
ISBN 978-0-919123-56-4. (1992) 128 pp. $25

THE BRILLIG TRILOGY:

  1. CHICKEN LITTLE: The Inside Story *(A Jungian romance)*
  ISBN 978-0-919123-62-5. (1993) 128 pp. $25

  2. WHO AM I, REALLY? Personality, Soul and Individuation
  ISBN 978-0-919123-68-7. (1995) 144 pp. $25

  3. LIVING JUNG: The Good and the Better
  ISBN 978-0-919123-73-1. (1996) 128 pp. $25

JUNGIAN PSYCHOLOGY UNPLUGGED: My Life as an Elephant
ISBN 978-0-919123-81-6. (1998) 160 pp. $25

DIGESTING JUNG: Food for the Journey
ISBN 978-0-919123-96-0. (2001) 128 pp. $25

JUNG UNCORKED: Rare Vintages from the Cellar of Jungian Psychology
Four vols.. ISBN 978-1-894574-21-1/22-8. (2008-2009) 128 pp. each. $25 each

THE SLEEPNOT TRILOGY:

  1. NOT THE BIG SLEEP: On having fun, seriously *(A Jungian romance)*
  ISBN 978-0-894574-13-6. (2005) 128 pp. $25

  2. ON STAYING AWAKE: Getting Older and Bolder *(Another Jungian romance)*
  ISBN 978-0-894574-16-7. (2006) 144 pp. $25

  3. EYES WIDE OPEN: Late Thoughts *(Another Jungian romance)*
  ISBN 978-0-894574-18-1. (2007) 160 pp. $25

THE EROS TRILOGY:

  1. LIVE YOUR NONSENSE: Halfway to Dawn with Eros (A Jungian Approach to
  Individuation). ISBN 978-0-894574-31-0. (2010) 128 pp. $25

  2. TRAMPLED TO DEATH BY GEESE: More Eros and a Lot More Nonsense (An Analyst's
  Perspective on the Inner Life). ISBN 978-0-894574-34-1. (20011) 160 pp. $25

  3. HIJACKED BY EROS: A Jungian analyst's picaresque adventures in the pleroma
  ISBN 978-0-894574-18-35-8. (2012) 128 pp. $25

MILES TO GO BEFORE I SLEEP: Growing Up Puer *(Another Jungian romance)*
ISBN 978-0-894574-36-5. (2013) 128 pp. $25